Bad

As I Wanna Be

Dennis

Rodman

with Tim Keown

Bad

As I Wanna Be

Delacorte Press

Published by
Delacorte Press
Bantam Doubleday Dell Publishing Group, Inc.
1540 Broadway
New York, New York 10036

"Alive"
Written by Eddie Vedder and Stone Gossard
© 1991 Innocent Bystander,
Write Treatage Music And Polygram International Publishing, Inc.

Library of Congress Cataloging in Publication Data
Rodman, Dennis, 1961–
    Bad as I wanna be / Dennis Rodman with Tim Keown.
       p.   cm.
    ISBN 0-385-31639-9
    1. Rodman, Dennis, 1961–   .   2. Basketball players—United
States—Biography.   I. Keown, Tim.   II. Title.
GV884.R618A3   1996
796.323′092—dc20
    [B]   96-5456
                                                                CIP

The trademark Delacorte Press® is registered in the U.S. Patent and
Trademark Office.

Book design by Susan Maksuta and Bonni Leon-Berman

Photo research by Photosearch Inc., New York

Manufactured in the United States of America

Published simultaneously in Canada

June 1996

10 9 8 7 6 5 4 3 2 1

BVG

Contents

Contents

ACKNOWLEDGMENTS

My deepest thanks to:

God—without you there'd be nothing.

Alexis—my daughter, I hope someday this book helps you understand your daddy. You are my inspiration for living, and I love you more than life.

Bryne Rich—for coming into my life. You are my best friend, and I love you.

Steve Ross—for his unbelievable vision and commitment to making this book a reality.

Howard Stern—for just being the cool dude who lives life his way.

Mike Silver—for being the first person to show the world who Dennis Rodman really is.

Tim Keown—for helping tell everyone how I feel and what I think more clearly than ever.

Richard Howell—attorney to the stars. Thanks for looking out for me.

Chicago Bulls—for accepting me for me, and letting me just do my job.

Chuck Daly—for being the one who showed me the way to becoming a man in the NBA.

James Rich—for showing me what character and truth are all about.

Mom and Debra and Kim—I love you all.

John Gianopolis—thanks for being there.

Pearl Jam—you guys do it like nobody else. Your music is a real inspiration.

Tammy Rodriquez—for all you've done to make me look good.

Dwight—Thanks for being a true friend. I know I don't say thanks much, but all that you've done for me has really made a difference in turning my life around. Thank you, thank you, thank you.

Is something
wrong
She said
Of course
there is
You're still
alive
She said
Do I deserve
to be
Is that the
question
And if so...
if so
Who answers?
Who answers?

—Pearl Jam
"Alive"

one

New and Improved

One Night, One Gun, One Decision

On an April night in 1993 I sat in the cab of my pickup truck with a rifle in my lap, deciding whether to kill myself. I was in the parking lot of The Palace of Auburn Hills, the site of many of my greatest moments as a professional basketball player for the Detroit Pistons. As I sat in the truck, looking out over the endless asphalt and the huge empty building, I discovered I was ready to check out of this life if it meant I could keep from being the man I was becoming.

I had two championship rings and was on my way to my second straight rebounding title. I had played in two All-Star Games and was the NBA Defensive Player of the Year twice. I was wildly popular in Detroit, the blue-collar workingman in a blue-collar workingman's town. I was the guy on the front line, taking the bullets for the troops, clearing the way for everyone else to get the glory. It was a role I loved, and a role the people loved to see me play.

I had all the material things everybody wants: a big house, a Ferrari, name recognition. I was a huge success story, a made-for-TV special in the living flesh. I had risen above a tough childhood, poor education, trouble with the law, and a stretch of homelessness. I was a black kid from the Oak Cliff project in Dallas who had been shown another side of life during college by a white Oklahoma farm family. My story read like fiction.

From the outside I had everything I could want. From the inside I had nothing but an empty soul and a gun in my lap.

Earlier that night I wrote a note to a friend of mine, Sheldon Steele, explaining how I was feeling at the time. I drove over to his house late that night, dropped off the note, and drove to the arena.

I don't remember exactly what the note said, but I was letting him know I wasn't sure I could continue on my current path. The note was personal, but it wasn't meant to be a suicide note. Later, it was reported to be one, but that wasn't my plan when I sat down and put the pen on the paper.

The rest of that night is crystal clear in my mind, and will be forever.

It wasn't unusual for me to drive out to the arena on nights when we didn't have a game. The arena is out in the middle of nowhere, with this huge parking lot that seems to go on forever. I would sometimes drive out there late at night or early in the morning and do some target shooting. Other times I went out there to work out in the Pistons' weight room.

I don't live my life by anybody else's clock. If I feel like doing something, I don't care what time it is. I just do it. Unless I absolutely have to be somewhere, time isn't a big factor for me. I don't wear a watch, I don't worry about what time it is, and I don't like to waste time sleeping. I know night and day, and that's about it. It was late when I left Sheldon's house, probably two or three in the morning, and I decided to go drive out to The Palace and get in a workout. I thought I could work some of the anxiety and pain out of my body by throwing some weights around and cranking Pearl Jam.

This happened near the end of my seventh and last season with the Pistons, and the team was going downhill fast. We ended up sixth in our division that season, with a 40–42 record, and we didn't even make the playoffs. That's pathetic when you consider we were world champions just three years before that. Our great team was being taken apart, piece by piece, and **I FELT LIKE MY LIFE WAS BEING TAKEN APART RIGHT WITH IT.**

There was nobody around when I got to the arena and let myself in. I worked out hard. I was working my body to the bone, lifting and listening to Pearl Jam. There was nobody else around, just me and the weights and the music. The place was like a fucking tomb. I tried to take those weights and throw everything at them, all the pain and sorrow that was running through my body.

When I listen to Pearl Jam, the music releases everything that's bound up inside me. It's hard for me to explain, but their music is so real, it makes me think about everything in my life. At that point I didn't need much encouragement. I was thinking enough already.

I was thinking a lot about how fucked up my life was, how much bullshit I was going through at the time, and **WONDERING HOW MUCH MORE I COULD TAKE.** I must have worked out for two hours before I closed the place, completely exhausted, and went back to the truck.

As I was walking out, I thought, *Fuck it. The gun's in the truck.* It was that simple. The whole time I was thinking that I shouldn't be doing this. I shouldn't be here. I shouldn't be an NBA player. This is all some fantasy world that I have no right to live in. I was just a kid from the projects who was always too skinny or too funny looking to be taken seriously. I was the kid they called the "Worm" because of the way I wiggled when I played pinball. Me, living this life, with women and money and attention everywhere? It didn't seem real.

The rifle was in the truck, under the seat. I turned Pearl Jam on the stereo and reached under the seat and grabbed the gun, wondering if I could do it. I knew right then I could; I could take that rifle and blow my fucking head off. There was that much pain. The life that might have looked so good from the outside was caving in on itself because **I couldn't continue to be the person everyone wanted me to be.**

I couldn't be what society wanted an athlete to be. I couldn't be the good soldier and the happy teammate and the good man off the court. **I tried, and I failed.** I tried marriage for the good of my child and had it blow up in my face. I tried to be loyal to my team and my teammates and had that explode when the organization began to tear the team apart. I tried to do all those things, all the right things, and I got nothing but pain and suffering in return.

Everyone was gone. My teammates were gone. My child was gone. My coach was gone. *I was alone, bro, all alone.* I was out there, exposed and hurt. It would seem to have been the lowest point in my life, but it didn't really feel that way. It felt to me like a standstill point. I felt stuck, paralyzed. I knew I could get the fame and the money, but how do you learn to deal with all the bullshit that comes with it? They don't teach you that part of it. You have to find it out for yourself, and that's what I was trying to do.

A lot of people say they wish they were dead, but how many of them really believe it? How many of them are really willing to act on it? Most of the time people are looking for pity or sympathy. I wasn't into that. I wouldn't have been sitting in the middle of a huge, empty parking lot at three in the morning if I was looking for attention. That was the last place I was going to get any attention.

I didn't want anybody else around. This was a battle with myself. Nobody else mattered. I just kept thinking, *This isn't me. This isn't Dennis Rodman. You're looking at somebody who's living somebody else's life.* I was sitting there wishing I could go to sleep and wake up in Dallas, back home—a normal, grind-it-out, nine-to-five guy, just like I was before any of this lightning struck in my life. I was burning a big hole in my soul, and for what? I had everything I wanted, but I was trying to be somebody I wasn't.

THE LIFE I WAS LEADING HAD CHANGED ME INTO SOMEBODY I DIDN'T EVEN KNOW.

As I sat there, I thought about my whole life, and how I was ready to cash it all in. *Just pull the trigger, bro,* and give it to somebody else. Pass on all those problems. There was some real pain there. I didn't know who I was or where I was going, and nobody seemed to understand that but me.

I thought about my father—the aptly named Philander Rodman—who left us when I was three years old and never came back. My mother says I used to walk around the house after he left, asking when Daddy was coming home. She knew the answer—never—but she always tried to keep me from being hurt by that truth.

I thought about my mother, Shirley, who raised me and my two younger sisters all by herself in the Oak Cliff projects in Dallas. There were times when we were hungry, many times, but she worked two and sometimes three jobs to keep us going.

I thought of a girl from Dallas named Lorita Westbrook, one of my sisters' friends, who convinced me to try out for the basketball team at Cooke County Junior College. I was twenty-one years old, working a part-time job cleaning cars at an Oldsmobile dealership. Six months earlier I'd been fired from my job as a graveyard-shift janitor at the Dallas-Fort Worth Airport for stealing fifty watches from an airport gift shop. **I was a nobody, just bumming around with some hoodlum buddies. Sometimes I'd walk the streets all night, knowing I had nowhere to stay.** I wasn't going to try out for this basketball team; what would I do in college?

But things were happening to me. STRANGE THINGS. Things that don't happen to anybody else. I had just grown an incredible amount—nine inches in the two years since I'd graduated from high school—but I still didn't think of myself as a basketball player.

I went from five foot eleven to six foot eight, and the more ball I played, the more I caught on to the game. I never had such confidence in anything before in my life—not schoolwork, not girls, not any other sport. All of a sudden I could do things on the basketball court that I'd never dreamed of doing. My sisters were always the ones with the basketball talent: Debra was an all-American at Louisiana Tech, Kim was an all-American at Stephen F. Austin. I was the runt of the family, living in their shadows, following them around until my hormones went crazy. It was like I had a new body that knew how to do all this shit the old one didn't.

There was a lot of pain and suffering in my childhood, but when I lay down in bed at night in that Oak Cliff project, I always had the same thought: **There's something big waiting out there for DENNIS RODMAN.** This wasn't logical thinking. I was a goofy kid who was so shy, I sometimes hid behind my mom in the grocery store. It didn't seem that anything major would ever happen to me, but I didn't think I was just kidding myself. I didn't think it was foolish kid stuff. I put reason aside and honestly believed I would be famous someday.

But I never thought of basketball as an outlet for me until I started growing and Lorita Westbrook saw me play and arranged that tryout at that little school in

Gainesville, Texas, about an hour's drive from the projects. Lorita had seen me play, and she had played at Cooke herself. Turns out she was a damned good talent scout.

Something made me go to that tryout. Maybe it had to do with those childhood dreams, but something pulled me to that school. For some reason I believed her. I guess somewhere inside me there was a part of me that believed in myself. I took it from there, with a few bumps in between, and made myself into an NBA player. I can honestly say I never had anything handed to me on my way to the NBA. **I CAME OUT OF NOWHERE, LIKE I DO WHEN I FLY IN FOR A REBOUND.** Nobody made me; I made myself.

But as I sat in the pickup, my confidence was gone. I wasn't sure of anything anymore. I was a guy with a gun in an empty parking lot. I thought a lot about how I got where I was, and how I wouldn't care if I had to go back. I wanted to be normal. The NBA life of adulation, money, and women was wearing me down. At that point I could have done without fame and money. As I sat in that pickup, I honestly thought I would have been happier back at that fucking airport, pushing a broom for $6.50 an hour.

I had a beautiful daughter who was four years old at the time—a daughter I rarely saw because of the nasty shit that followed my divorce from my ex-wife, Annie. The marriage was a mistake in the first place; it lasted only eighty-two days and created a lot of pain and suffering that I still feel. **I got burned, in a bad way.**

Basketball was always my release from those problems. We won the NBA Finals two years in a row with the Pistons, and we were still a pretty young team after our second title. We were the "Bad Boys" and we lived up to our name. Some guys were getting older, but the core—Isiah Thomas, Joe Dumars, Bill Laimbeer, John Salley, me—were still young enough to have a few good years together. I thought we were set for a while—I thought I could stay there my whole career, really—but that went away, too. First, Rick Mahorn left. Then Vinnie Johnson and James Edwards and Salley. Laimbeer wasn't playing very much, and all of a sudden the team was falling apart and there weren't enough guys around to pick up the slack. I looked around and figured, *Okay, I'm next in line to leave*—and I was right. By then, the "Bad Boys" were like something from a history book.

When we were winning championships, Chuck Daly used to sit us down and say, **"Remember these times. It'll never get any better."** He was right. Man, was he ever right. Those teams had everything: power, finesse, brains. We could beat the ugly shit out of the other team or be pretty about it. It didn't matter, bro: you pick how you want to lose, because we didn't care how we beat you.

Those times were gone. When Daly left after the 1991–92 season, he took the heart of the team with him. That man had taught me more than anyone in the world about basketball, and what it took to win in the NBA. When he left Detroit, it was like they pulled my anchor out of the water.

All of this was running through my mind—personal problems, professional problems, everything. **I was two people: *ONE PERSON ON THE INSIDE*, another person on the outside.** The person I wanted to kill was the person on the outside. The guy on the inside was fine, he just wasn't getting out much. The guy on the inside was normal, even though he had a lot of money and fame. The guy on the outside was all fucked up, not knowing what he wanted.

I came up with an idea: *Fuck the gun. Why not just kill the guy on the outside and let the other one keep living*? I already knew I could pull the trigger if I wanted. If that was some kind of test, I'd already passed it in my mind. I was searching for a way to come to grips with that person I didn't want to be. I wanted to get that part out of my life and let the other one out to breathe.

And if I got rid of that life, what options did I have? I could have gone off and been a nine-to-five guy who would have been happier and would have had fewer problems. My bank account would have suffered, but I would have been able to walk the streets as a normal person. That's all I was looking for. The other option I considered was to keep doing what I was doing and try to fool people into believing I was something that I wasn't.

Then I thought of a third option: Live a normal life, stay true to myself, and stay exactly where I am.

I sat in that pickup and had a duel with myself. I didn't need the gun; it all took place in my mind. I walked one way and I walked the other way. ***At ten paces I turned and shot the impostor.*** I killed the Dennis Rodman that had tried to conform to what everybody wanted him to be.

The choice I had to make was this: Did I want to be like almost everyone else in the NBA and be used and treated as a product for other people's profit and enjoyment? Or did I want to be my own person, be true to myself and let the person inside me be free to do what he wanted to do, no matter what anybody else said or thought?

In that parking lot I realized I could do both things at once. I could be a successful and prominent basketball player and stay true to myself. This was a huge turning point in my life. At that point I could have gone through with it. I could have pulled the trigger, but that would have been the easy way, the cheap way. Instead, I dealt with it and solved the problem.

When I realized I could turn my back on everything teammates say and coaches say and society says, I felt free. It was like I came out from under the water and took a deep breath.

After that I went to sleep. Everything after that is something of a blur. I WOKE UP WITH A COUPLE POLICE OFFICERS AT MY WINDOW; Sheldon had called the police, thinking I was really going to kill myself. Those guys were wondering what the hell was going on. The gun was on the seat next to me, and I was sleeping like a tired dog.

Once it was over, it wasn't a big deal to me. I'd had my crisis, come to my conclusions, and gone to sleep. But the

Pistons thought differently. **They wanted to put me in the hospital.** They wanted to give me some time off. They thought I'd gone way off the deep end.

When they told me about going to the hospital, I said, "Nah. I'm cool, bro. It was no big deal."

They said they at least wanted me to see a psychiatrist, so I did that. Right away, that morning. We talked about what I had done and why I'd done it. We talked about the things that were running through my head, and why I thought this life was pulling me apart. I told him the whole story and how I took care of it.

This went on for a while, and finally the psychiatrist looked up at me and said, "There's nothing wrong with you."

"I know that," I said. **"There's nothing wrong with me at all."**

Death has always had a prominent place in my mind. I've thought about killing myself, and there are times when **I THINK SOMEBODY MIGHT KILL ME.** That's part of fame—dealing with the reality that somebody might dislike you enough to come after you. It's a wild notion, but I think everybody in my position feels the same thing, to one degree or another. With me it's more of a factor because I live so hard, and I live so open. I'm not afraid of death. I'm not going to stop doing the things I do—going out to clubs, riding my motorcycle, going out on my power boat—just because there might be a risk involved.

But if I had killed myself that night, I know what would have happened. People would have thought I had been sending out all these warning signals, that I was deranged and needed help. They would have said they'd seen it coming a mile away, that I was nothing more than a bas-

ketball-playing time bomb. There would have been specu-
lation that I was on drugs, even though I'm the most
antidrug guy who ever stepped onto an NBA court.

When a high-profile personality lives like I do, always
looking for a new experience or a new challenge, everybody thinks that person is fated to die young.

What I did that night in The Palace parking lot—the
choice I made and the way I made it—allowed me to
break out and become the person I am today. I made the
decision that night: *Follow your own brain*. Because of that
night the Dennis Rodman you see now is a prototype,
**THE ONE YOU SHOULD HAVE BEEN SEEING
ALL ALONG.**

two

Nobody from Nowhere

A Janitor Makes It Big

The Texas State Fair is held in Dallas, about five miles from where I grew up in the Oak Cliff projects. None of the kids I hung around with had enough money to get into the fair, but we went every year.

There is an underground sewage tunnel that can take you right there. We'd crawl in through a manhole in the project and start our journey. This tunnel was legendary among kids in Oak Cliff; I think everyone who grew up there went to the state fair that way at one time or another. My friends and I started taking this route when I was thirteen or fourteen.

The tunnel was wide in most places, but it stunk like you wouldn't believe. The sewage was about a foot deep, so we had to walk around it, sort of on the side of the tunnel. It was dark and scary, so we'd bring flashlights so we could work our way around the crap and also so we could follow the lines that somebody had drawn years ago to mark the way.

When I think back on it, I just shake my head. **Five miles through a sewage tunnel to the state fair? What kind of crazy mess was that?** Other kids were driving in their parents' cars, probably getting all kinds of money to ride the rides and buy cotton candy. We were walking around shit, holding our noses, trying to find the arrows with the beam of a flashlight. This was summer in Dallas, hotter than hell. In some places the tunnel got real narrow, and we'd have to crawl through with the sewage right in our noses. It was dark as night in there, and if you weren't the one holding the flashlight, you could end up getting your hands or face into something you didn't want.

The tunnel took us right into the middle of the state fair. There was a manhole cover right inside. I wonder about the first guy who went through there and found out where it came out. What the fuck was he thinking? You should have seen the looks on people's faces when we would climb the ladder and lift off the manhole cover. We'd pop our heads out like groundhogs, squinting in the sun. Nobody ever bothered with us, though; maybe they thought anybody who would put themselves through that deserves a little fun.

That's what we had to do for fun: walk and crawl and run through a small stream

Me at six (center), with cousins Dwight and Reggie

of sewage for five miles. I think back to times like that and realize how easy everything is for me now. **I THINK THAT'S WHY I STRIVE TO MAKE MY LIFE SO DIFFICULT NOW. I'M NOT COMFORTABLE BEING COMFORTABLE.** I struggled so much when I was learning to make my way, and now I think back and say, "Shit, that was difficult, but you know what? It was damn fun." I'm totally reverting back to those times now, trying to recapture that spirit. **I CAN'T BE MR. GLAMOROUS, I'M-TOO-FUCKING-GOOD-FOR-YOU.** I can't be that way.

I like to describe my life as a black hole with a little light out there. I'm trying to get at that light, just like we tried to get at the light that would get us into the state fair. That light keeps moving, and it brings new challenges.

Everyone has to find the right tunnel. It was hard for me. I walked through a lot of tunnels, made a lot of wrong turns, before I got to the right place. In a lot of ways I'm still that same little kid, crawling through that tunnel on my way to the state fair.

When I was three my father stopped coming home.

I never really knew my father, Philander Rodman. He was in the Air Force in New Jersey, where I was born, and when I was three we packed up and came back to Dallas, where my mother is from. We did this when my father stopped coming home.

My father isn't part of my life. I haven't seen him in more than thirty years, so what's there to miss? I just look at it like this: Some man brought me into this world. That doesn't mean I have a father; I don't. I could say, "This is my father. This is my dad," but that doesn't sound right to me. I grew up with my mother and two younger sisters, Debra and Kim. There wasn't a male role model in my life until I got to college and started getting my shit together.

A lot of times you'll hear somebody ask an NBA player what he'd be doing if he wasn't getting paid to play basketball. The answer they get pretty often is: **DEAD OR IN JAIL.** Most of us are from shitty backgrounds: projects, ghettos, no money, no father, no hope. I think that's a big reason a lot of guys make it—they're escaping through basketball. Sometimes guys say "Dead or in jail" because it sounds good and makes them out to be tougher than they really are. But with me I think it's true—and I have the evidence.

I was homeless for about six months when I was nineteen, during the time I was growing like a weed. I was living in Dallas, not going to school, not really doing anything with my life. My mom was having a hard time providing for everybody, and here she had this deadbeat nineteen-year-old son sitting around the house not doing much of anything. My sisters were seventeen and eighteen, and they were the pride of the family anyway with their basketball and school, so I was pretty much in the way.

My sisters had a gift then—basketball—that I didn't have until later. They were both stars at our high school, South Oak Cliff, and they both became college all-Americans. They were tall and strong—Debra was six foot two, Kim six feet. I was supportive of what they were doing, but I was kind of in the background and I got teased about it. Now it's completely turned around; they're completely blown away by what I've done. To them I'm just their crazy brother, but you know what? My sister Debra, the next oldest, has three tattoos. She never had any before.

My mom didn't want to kick me out of the house, but I could tell she didn't want me hanging around either. She

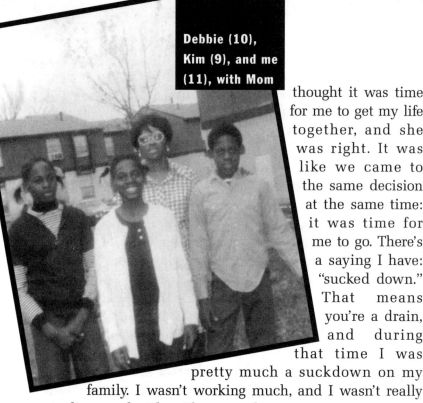

Debbie (10), Kim (9), and me (11), with Mom

thought it was time for me to get my life together, and she was right. It was like we came to the same decision at the same time: it was time for me to go. There's a saying I have: "sucked down." That means you're a drain, and during that time I was pretty much a suckdown on my family. I wasn't working much, and I wasn't really stealing much either. That came later.

The problem was, I didn't have anywhere to go. I was out on the streets, just hanging. I went from house to house, staying with friends, maybe sleeping on their floor or a couch. Many nights I just walked all night, going nowhere, roaming the streets of Oak Cliff like a lost soul. Other times my friends would walk with me; three or four of us would just hang out and stay awake all night, then sleep during the day. Some nights I just slept on the streets.

I got into a lot of shit living in the projects. That goes with the territory. You stay out late, have a fun time, do whatever you want. When I was there, Oak Cliff was like a big cubbyhole, with everybody trying to look after everybody else. I think it's broken down some since I was there, but back then people knew if they lost sight of someone, they'd stray. And then they'd be gone forever, eaten up by the streets.

The fact I was homeless at one time is part of why I can relate to people out there who are going through hard times. It's why I can go into a tough part of town and have a real conversation with somebody standing on the corner

16

begging for change. It's why they see me as a real person and not some image that somebody in the NBA office created. **I've been homeless. I've worked at 7-Eleven.** I'm a real person, with real experiences, and I know how easy it is to find yourself out there with nothing. Who knows—I sometimes think **it might happen to me again someday.**

During the time I was on the street, I was noticing how much I was growing. It was unbelievable. I was about five foot eleven—maybe—when I graduated from high school. I was like all kids, measuring myself on the kitchen wall and always saying, **"MAN, I WISH I WAS TALLER."** Especially since my sisters were so damned tall. I wondered when it was going to be my turn. Then I got out of high school—when nobody grows—and I started noticing it. It felt like every day I was growing. I was thinking, **Wait a minute.** I didn't know what was going on. It seemed like everything was happening to me at once. I was confused and didn't really understand what the hell my body was doing. I guess it went back to what I always believed: There was something in store for Dennis Rodman down the road. At the time I didn't know what it was. I sort of found out by accident.

I decided I had to get a job and make something of myself. I was twenty years old, and there was nothing going on in my life. I went to the Dallas-Fort Worth Airport and got a job as a janitor on the graveyard shift. This job has become a big part of the Rodman legend. I can't believe how often it comes up, just because it's so damn different than most NBA players. At the time I didn't think it was a big deal. I was pushing a broom or mopping the floors for $6.50 an hour, which wasn't bad money for me back then. I was just working, just like everybody else in the world. There was no reason for me to believe I'd ever do much more than that.

I'D BEEN STEALING STUFF FOR A WHILE. Petty stuff. A cheap wallet here, a few bucks there, maybe something from a convenience store. Then one night at the airport I was pushing a broom around and I found I could steal these watches out of a closed gift shop by reaching the broom handle through the metal slats in the gate. There was nobody around, so I decided to do it. It was a kick, a challenge, and before I was finished I **had fifty fucking watches in my pockets.**

Fifty watches. I don't know what the fuck I was thinking, bro. Some of them were cheap, but some were worth around fifty dollars. It was like nothing, it was so easy. I was big time now. I had these watches, and nobody would ever find out.

I didn't want those watches. I couldn't have cared less about those watches. If I was going to steal something for myself, it sure as hell wouldn't have been something to use to tell time. I just took them to take them—no reason other than the kick of stealing—and then I decided I could give them to all my friends. **I wanted them to think I was a big shot.** I wanted them to walk around saying, "Son of a bitch, that guy can get anything he wants."

I wanted them to know if they ever needed anything, all they had to do was come and ask Dennis. *People didn't accept me* as much of anything at that time. This would be my new role, my niche. Sometimes I got the feeling doing wrong was expected of us where we came from. Everyone did it, so why not me? It was monkey see, monkey do. I just gave in and became a thief to be accepted. I was going to use that as a way of getting out of the mess.

I didn't know they had hidden cameras in that goddamn gift shop. I went out and gave every one of those watches away. I gave them to my friends, my mom, my sisters—even to some people I really didn't know that well. Just handed them out. Nobody seemed to wonder what the hell was going on. They were just, "A new watch? Cool." I felt big then.

Then the airport police showed up at my mom's house and told her they were looking for me. They'd looked at the films and had me dead to rights. They arrested me and put me in the airport jail.

In jail I was just like everybody else. I WAS SITTING THERE PRAYING, feeling caged. I went through the whole routine: God, I'll never do anything like this again; if I can only go home, I'll straighten up and never be back here. It was the same ritual everybody goes through when they get in trouble, the same pitiful shit.

I sat there and was honest with myself. "This is no kind of life. Something's got to happen." I think I made the decision right there that I couldn't continue to live like that. I guess it was time to see if all those childhood fantasies of making it big were true or just bullshit.

My mother decided to let me stay in there for a night, to teach me a lesson. It was a tough night. The next day she couldn't take it anymore, and neither could I, so she bailed me out. I gave the police all the names of the people who had the watches, and they went around and rounded up the stolen watches. They got every last one of them.

They would go up to these people and ask, "Dennis Rodman give you this watch?"

"Yeah."

"He sell it to you?"

"Nah, he just gave it to me."

The cops must have wondered what the fuck was up with me. What kind of criminal is this, bro? I didn't make a dime off any of the watches. I didn't even try to. I just passed them out, **looking for acceptance,** trying to be a big fucking deal in the neighborhood.

Once they recovered all the watches, they dropped the charges. I was going up the stairs of the courthouse, nervous as shit, when my lawyer came out and told me to go home and forget about it. Nobody who got a watch put up a fight—they just kind of laughed and handed them over. Once they got all the watches, they didn't care about me. They were cool with that, but two weeks later they called me in and fired me from the job.

They told me if they hadn't gotten all the watches back **I WAS LOOKING AT SIX MONTHS IN JAIL.**

In places like Oak Cliff stealing and dealing are the ways out. It's the way you get to be cool and noticed. There was nobody around there to look up to, because once people make something of themselves, they move out.

I started playing basketball more seriously after I got caught stealing the watches. I was just playing with friends in a gym, and that's where Lorita Westbrook saw me play. It was night leagues or pickup games; mostly, I was just hanging at the gym, like a kid with a new toy. I was getting close to six eight by this time, and even though I was skinny and a little embarrassed by the growth spurt, it was like I had a new body. *I could do things on the basketball court that weren't possible before.*

The only time I'd played organized basketball was my sophomore year in high school, when I barely made the junior varsity team and quit halfway through the season. I was just a little nervous kid who never got into the game, and I couldn't handle that. Just like now, I had way too much energy to sit on the bench.

I don't know where Lorita Westbrook is today, but I bet she tells everyone she discovered Dennis Rodman. I went to that tryout at Cooke County Junior College and after about fifteen minutes they pulled me aside and told me they had a scholarship for me. All this happened way too fast. I don't know if I was ready to start a basketball career at twenty-one years old, but I was going there anyway. By that time, **IT WAS LIKE THE WHOLE THING WAS OUT OF MY CONTROL.**

I played only 16 games for Cooke County. I flunked out after a semester and figured it was all a waste of time. I could have made up the work, but I didn't bother. I averaged more than 17 points and 13 rebounds at Cooke—not bad for a guy who had never really played any organized basketball. The talent was there, but the rest of the package hadn't come together.

I went back to bumming in Dallas. I was hanging with the same old guys, but I never got deeper into crime than the occasional petty theft. One of my friends was a big-time drug dealer, and some of the other guys worked for him. I was back to wandering between my mother's house and the streets, doing no good. Back to the same old shit.

Lonn Reisman, an assistant coach at Southeastern Oklahoma—an NAIA school—had seen me play while I was at Cooke, and he was convinced I could make it. He talked to the head coach, Jack Hedden, and they decided to come after me. They were determined, too, because I didn't want anything to do with college after that one semester. Coaches would call when I was at my mother's house and I'd refuse to take the calls. I didn't want to hear what they had to say. The only reason I talked to Hedden and Reisman is because **they showed up at the house one day and I answered the door.**

I don't know for sure, but I'd guess this isn't the way Shaquille O'Neal's college recruiting went. Or Michael Jordan, or anybody else in the whole NBA. When you look at how I got placed in the position to do what I've done— the girl convincing me to try out, everybody giving those watches back, then me answering the door when some coaches were there—you'll probably agree **somebody was looking out for me.** I don't know who, and I don't know why, but somebody was.

Those coaches convinced me I could go there and make something of myself. I think I had already convinced myself of something too: I needed to get out of Dallas, for good. I needed to leave all that street crap in my past and move on with my life. **I was going nowhere in a BIG HURRY.**

Southeastern Oklahoma University is in Durant, Oklahoma, a town of about six thousand people. Compared to what I was used to, Durant was a different world, bro. A whole different world.

It wasn't easy for a guy like me, who didn't know anything besides the city. All I ever knew was the city and the projects, and that didn't prepare me for what I got up there in that small town.

I noticed the difference right away. I was walking to class soon after I got there, and some asshole leaned his head out of the car window and yelled, "You go home, you black son of a bitch." That happened a lot. **They'd tell me, "Get your black ass out of here," or "Go back to Africa, nigger."**

There were many times when I wanted to get back at those people, when I wanted to deal with it the only way I knew how: with violence.

I didn't, though. I didn't because there was a little kid there, telling me not to.

The little kid was named Bryne Rich. I had met Bryne at the Southeastern basketball camp the summer before I started school there. He was thirteen and I was twenty-two. I can remember him looking at me funny, which wasn't unusual; back in those days, **I SOMETIMES WALKED AROUND WITH QUARTERS IN MY EARS.** I don't know why I did it—probably just **SO PEOPLE WOULD THINK I WAS CRAZY.** Anyway, Bryne and I became friends—best friends.

Bryne kind of fell in love with me at that camp. He invited me over to his house for dinner, and I went. It was weird. I remember saying, **"Why is this kid in love with me? Why does he love me so damn much?"**

The Riches lived in Bokchito, about fifteen miles from Durant. Before long I lived there too. Bokchito is tiny, bro, much smaller than Durant. There isn't much there but dirt roads and a few farms. The Riches had a farm and Bryne's father, James, also worked for the post office. I had a room in a dormitory on campus, but I moved in there because Bryne and I hit it off. It seemed like the thing to do.

Bryne and I had something in common from the start, as strange as it seems. **We were both coming off HARD TIMES, and we were both confused about stuff in our lives.** I was trying to decide where my life was going, and Bryne was trying to deal with having shot and killed his best friend in a freak hunting accident the year before. Bryne told his parents he wanted a little brother. He got me instead.

I think we came together at the right time for both of us. It was a real heartwarming story. I had to fight through a lot of racist bullshit living out there, and they helped me get through it. It was such an unreal scene: **me**, who never knew anything but the projects, living with this white family, **getting up at five in the morning to milk cows or do some other chore.**

These were people who had never dealt with a black person before, and they weren't totally comfortable with it. Bryne's mom, Pat, had the hardest time. She was taking classes at Southeastern, and she used to hide from me when I went looking for her to give me a ride back to the farm. **SHE WAS WORRIED ABOUT WHAT PEOPLE WOULD THINK** or say if they saw her with this big black man. Sometimes she would take the back way home, going way around all the main streets so nobody would see me in the car with her.

I used to make fun of it. I'd say, "Mrs. Rich, why you going this way?" I knew why she was doing it, but I played dumb. It didn't make me feel any less welcome at their house, though. It was all about image in a small community. People actually thought I was sleeping with her.

These people didn't know anything about black people, so the only thing they could imagine was the worst thing.

They thought, *Why is he with that boy's mother?*

Sometimes they thought Bryne was my son.

I think the experience made me stronger. I learned a lot I wouldn't have learned roaming the streets in Dallas, that's for sure. I think I showed her a side of life she would have never known too. Over the course of a couple years she realized what I was all about. She understood I was part of the family and she treated me like that.

They're one of the major reasons I got to where I am. I don't know what would have happened if I would have had to deal with all that bullshit there by myself.

There were so many times I had a shotgun in my hand—or near enough—when those people would call me a nigger or tell me to go back to Africa. I wanted to shoot somebody so many times. I kept a shovel in the car the Riches let me use, and one time I came close to taking it and banging a guy's head in after he yelled some crap. There were a lot of things I could have done, but the little kid said no.

Bryne said no. A lot of things could have stopped Dennis Rodman from being who he is today, and that's one of them. If Bryne hadn't been with me a lot of those times, I probably would have ended up in jail. I probably would have used that shovel on that guy's head. I didn't know any other way to handle crap like that.

The easy way to do things is to cop out and do the worst shit in the world. Then you don't have to worry about being successful. The easiest thing for me to do would have been to use that shovel, or use that gun. That would have been a copout. Then I could have failed and had an excuse.

Bryne is still my best friend. He helps to run my construction company—Rodman Excavation in Frisco, Texas—and we talk all the time. We both went through a lot together, and that's a strong bond.

When I lived with the Riches, I had to work for everything. I had to get up at five and feed cows, put sick cows back in the barn—all that farm business. It didn't matter whether I had a game that night or not.

I didn't go to a school that gave athletes every break. I had a C average in school, but I didn't get anything handed to me. There was some special treatment that came from being an athlete, but none of it showed up in the classroom. If I flunked, I flunked. I didn't get any gift grades, just like I didn't get any money handed to me or a free car to drive.

Just look at guys like Chris Washburn and William Bedford, first-round draft picks in the NBA who bombed out because they couldn't stay away from drugs. Guys like that get into trouble in the league their first few years because they're not used to doing anything on their own. I had my own set of problems when I got into the league—problems that had to do with getting so much after having so little—but all the hard work made me tough minded.

NAIA all-American 3 years in row

Eventually, I was accepted in the community at Southeastern because I could play basketball. That's when I first saw the power and the bullshit that comes with having a little notoriety. I was the best player they'd ever seen in that area—I was an NAIA all-American three years in a row, averaged more than 25 points and 15 rebounds in my career, led the NAIA in rebounding twice, took the team to the NAIA championship my junior year—so they let me slide.

That was the first time I was able to see through people, into what they were really thinking. ***I knew I would have been just another nigger if I didn't play basketball.*** You would have had to be dead not to see that.

What they were saying is, "We don't mind if you're black, as long as you can play good basketball."

A lot of white people can relate to me now, and they can accept me now, but they wouldn't have accepted that struggling little kid I used to be. They wouldn't have accepted that guy who was wandering the streets, or the guy who lifted the watches, or the guy who dropped out of school. You're not going to pay attention to somebody who isn't going to "make it." Society allows itself to put that stuff behind and say, "Okay, you're accepted now, Dennis, because you've got a lot of money. You're accepted because you're famous, and we like having you around."

When I was twenty, those people would have crossed the street to get away from me. Now they're crowding around, trying to get an autograph. It's bullshit—and I can see right through it.

Them was always someone there for me, and in Oklahoma it was James Rich. It wasn't somebody with a lot of money or a lot of fame, it was a farmer who delivered mail for a living. A regular person. He was the one who looked at me when I screwed up and said, "Hey, you can't do that. You came from the projects, you came from the streets, but this isn't the streets. **You want to go back to the streets?"**

When I first got there, I used to look at him and say, "Yeah, I do."

"Tough," he said. "I'm not going to let you."

That man brought out the human side of me. He made me a better person. He never let me get too far out of line. He never let me stray. He didn't preach to me or anything, he just set everything out and told me this was the way it was going to be. I had to work, I had to help out, and I had to behave. I learned a lot from this man—a man who didn't get past the sixth grade.

He was like an old wise man in a fairy tale. I couldn't believe this man was in my life. I couldn't believe a man like that existed. He just laid it all out on the line and let me know I could make something out of myself if I wanted to face up to reality. There was no cloud over any of it; it was straight to the point, clear as day.

He looked at everything straight ahead. Everything was on a line from one point to the next. He wasn't the type who would sit down and tell me I could be a famous basketball player if I wanted it bad enough. He wouldn't fill my head with that stuff, because it wasn't really his style. Instead, he would say, **"Whatever you do, make it positive. Make it what you want it to be, not what somebody else wants it to be."**

When I left Dallas, I left everything that went with it. I cut it off, because I thought the only way I could make it was to turn my back on everything in my past. I had to forget in order to move on. I had to remove the distractions.

I put my mind forward and decided to make it, and I left a lot behind—even my mother. My mother worked real hard to get us what we needed when we were growing up, and I appreciate that. I've done a lot for her—bought her a house, bought her cars—but we're not that close. We have sort of a weird relationship; sometimes we talk twice a week, other times we won't talk for a month. I'm not real close with my sisters either. We talk sometimes, and I know what's going on in their lives, but I left a lot of myself back there when I left. It hasn't been the same since.

The way I look at it, I had no choice. My family probably took it the wrong way when I got close with the Rich family and started considering them my real family. I just had to break away from everything that was holding me back.

From the time you're a little kid in the projects, you're told to improve yourself, work hard and get out of there. You're a success if you can leave all that behind. But when a black person achieves that success and leaves the projects and everything else behind, they get criticized for forgetting their roots. You forget where you came from, everybody says.

I DON'T FORGET MY ROOTS.

I never have. I always go back and drive through or walk through Oak Cliff when I'm down there. I visualized what happened there and what I did to overcome it. I go back there for perspective, because sometimes I need it. *It keeps me hungry and keeps me grounded.*

After my senior year at Southeastern I was like this sideshow for the NBA. They looked at my statistics, and they looked at my age (by then I was twenty-five), and they didn't know what to make of me. They loved my body and my speed—they all kept saying I could have made the Olympics in the 400 meters—but they weren't sure I had the right game for the NBA.

Everywhere I went, they kept throwing out the same word: project. They saw me as someone who might be worth taking a chance on, because you never knew how it would pay off later.

I didn't care what they called me, just so somebody gave me a chance. I went into the postseason All-Star tournaments like a man possessed. The coaches at Southeastern told me I could play in the NBA, but I don't think too many other people did. Then I was the MVP of the Portsmouth Invitational in Virginia, one of the big showcases for guys coming out of college, and that opened a lot of eyes.

THERE WERE A LOT OF BIG-NAME PLAYERS IN THOSE TOURNAMENTS, AND I KICKED EVERYBODY'S ASS. It was the same as always, me playing harder than everybody else. Being hungrier. Now, the big-name college players don't even have to go to those tournaments. They think it's a waste of time because they've established themselves from before their college season even starts, and their agents and coaches tell them, "Don't go there. You might get hurt."

If you're that fucking good, go there and show it. Forget about getting hurt. Go in with all the other great athletes and let people know you're ready to compete.

The Pistons took me in the second round of the 1986 draft. I was the twenty-seventh player taken that year. I went behind guys like Kenny Walker, Brad Sellers, and Johnny Dawkins. ***The guy who went one pick before me*** was Greg Dreiling, a seven-foot center from Kansas who **averaged 2.2 points** and **2.2 rebounds** in his NBA career. **I guess they can say he's consistent.**

I came right into a team with Isiah Thomas, Adrian Dantley, Bill Laimbeer, Vinnie Johnson, Rick Mahorn—that team was set. They knew I was going to bring some energy to the team, but they probably didn't think they'd get anything out of me for a long time. If at all. Remember, bro, I was a project, someone who needed a couple years of solid work before making a mark in the league.

One thing, though: I was a project on a mission. I was willing to do anything to stay in the league. I was different, an outsider, but I wanted to hang around as long as I could. I came at things from a different angle, because I knew what I had left behind. I knew how hard it had been to get there in the first place.

I loved coming in as the guy nobody had ever heard of. I didn't care. During my first training camp with the Pistons, a reporter came up to me after a practice and said, **"WHO ARE YOU?"** I looked up at this dude and said: **"I'm nobody, straight out of nowhere."**

three

Wild Ride

The Pistons Do It Right

I made news right away in Detroit. The day I signed my contract, I hyperventilated and had to see the team doctor. **I guess I wasn't always as cool as I am now.**

I was sick during the week leading up to that first day in Detroit, and I don't really remember exactly what happened that day—or why. I do know I was very excited about being there. I had finally achieved something I worked so hard to achieve, and—combined with being sick—I guess I just got overwhelmed and hyperventilated.

This is just what Chuck Daly and the Pistons management expected of me. They saw a kid who wanted to make it—bad. They saw a wild, crazy young guy coming from nowhere who would do anything to have a career in the league. They weren't sure how good I would be right away, but they knew they had someone who would dive on the floor, throw his body everywhere, do whatever the team needed.

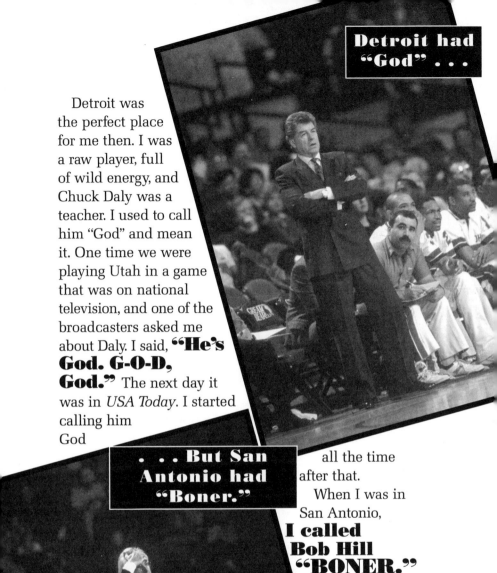

Detroit was the perfect place for me then. I was a raw player, full of wild energy, and Chuck Daly was a teacher. I used to call him "God" and mean it. One time we were playing Utah in a game that was on national television, and one of the broadcasters asked me about Daly. I said, **"He's God. G-O-D, God."** The next day it was in *USA Today*. I started calling him God

. . . But San Antonio had "Boner."

all the time after that.

When I was in San Antonio, **I called Bob Hill "BONER."** You can probably guess that I didn't feel the same way about Bob Hill as I did Chuck Daly.

Chuck Daly and the Pistons gave me a shot. They felt the team was coming together

33

with a bunch of veterans and badass inside players, and they figured they might as well give me a chance. My style fit in well with what they were trying to do, and if it worked out it could be great for both sides. The Pistons could have another piece to a championship puzzle and I could finish ***my wild ride from nowhere.***

The NBA was like this new world for me. I was very immature, and I'd never seen a stage even close to this big. I had some money, women—you name it, the door was open. I won't say I didn't experience what was out there. **I SPENT MONEY, I SLEPT WITH WOMEN AROUND THE LEAGUE, BUT I ALWAYS KEPT MY MIND ON THE GAME.** I was always looking for a way to give myself that edge, to put my mind back to the times when I was suffering and needed to rely on myself just to survive. I didn't want to get too hung up on all the possibilities out there and forget what I was there to do: play the fucking game.

I didn't play much my rookie year. I sat on the bench trying to keep all the energy inside. That killed me. I played in 77 of the 82 games, but I averaged only fifteen minutes a game. Those five games I didn't play at all drove me nuts. When I got out on the floor, I was wild. I wanted to do everything at once and show them I needed to play. I did need to play, but I needed to play because ***I was going* BAT-SHIT *sitting on the bench.***

Chuck Daly liked me right off, and he always told me my time would come. I think he liked seeing a guy who was just so fresh, who wasn't some top-dog college player unwilling to work and expecting everything handed to his ass on a silver platter. He always told me to keep my head together and everything would work out.

That was a great team to learn from. When I was a rookie, Rick Mahorn told me, "I'm going to teach you how it's done, bro." Those guys had the right attitude, and they saw I had something they needed. I was physical like Mahorn and Laimbeer, but I was faster than shit and could guard anybody in the league. I was like a new product, something the NBA had never seen before.

After my rookie year I decided I needed to do something to make a spot for myself in the league. I saw a lot of guys who sat at the end of the bench for a couple years, never doing anything to stand out, then end up getting tossed out of the league.

After everything I had gone through to get there, there was no way in hell I was going to let it slip away without putting up a fight.

I figured I made it to the league the hard way, so why not stay in it the hard way too? The hard way in the NBA is through defense and rebounding—the two things guys would rather not do. There's not a guy in the league, besides me, who doesn't want to score. That's why nobody can believe me: **I DON'T WANT TO SCORE.**

I was playing Adrian Dantley every day in practice, and I set out to make his life miserable. I was going to shut him down if it meant dying out there on the practice floor. I shut him down a few times, then he'd score on me. It went like that for a while, but then I realized I was shutting him down a lot more than he was scoring.

In the middle of my second season Dantley hurt his ankle and Daly put me into the starting lineup. We were over .500 when Dantley went down, but we took off with me in the lineup. **Of the first 24 games I started, we won 20. We just beat people up,** and Daly played me all over the court. I played the small forward mostly, but he'd put me inside against the power forwards and outside against the tough shooting guards. Wherever we needed defense, that's where I was.

I think it was during that stretch that the people of Detroit started getting into the phenomenon of the

"Worm." It was pretty amazing for me to see that nickname that I'd been given as a little kid, for the way I wiggled when I played pinball, splashed across headlines in the Detroit papers. The people were into what I was giving them, because it was so fresh and exciting. They knew basketball, and they appreciated my style. I looked to score some that year—it was my career-high 11.6-per-game year—but there were still times when I'd get an offensive rebound and dribble all the way out beyond the three-point line and give the damn thing to Isiah.

I started to become a star in that town, just by being the way I was. It was natural. It was the way I played in college, so I didn't see it as anything different. But people like to see someone rise up and make it. They feel they have more of a connection to that person. I was up for all of it. The media loved me because I would give them whatever they wanted. **I would say WILD SHIT,** whatever came to mind, and they started hanging out by my locker after games—even if I didn't do anything in the game. Mitch Albom, a columnist from the *Detroit Free Press*, used to come over to my house and play music with me. I played the drums and he played the piano.

With the Pistons, and with Chuck Daly, it was enough that I was playing the game the way I knew how. All out. All the time. That's the way I still play. Daly appreciated that, and so did the people of Detroit. It got to the point where I was the most popular player on that team. I wasn't flashy like Isiah, but **I gave them the BLOOD, SWEAT, and TEARS they wanted.**

They loved me there because I was like them. I was like a factory worker who went to work every day and performed in a role you couldn't do without. **Those people would go to work and maybe put bolts on a car door. But if you asked them what they did for a living, they'd tell you they made cars.**

Not tightened bolts—built cars. With me, I didn't just rebound or hustle my ass off—**I won basketball games.**

When I first got to Detroit, before our championship run, things were bad in the city. Auto factories were closing and a lot of people were out of work. It was totally horrible and depressing in Detroit back in 1986 and '87. **Sometimes I think people take sports too seriously, but I do believe we did some good for that city.** When we started winning, the whole aura of the place picked up with us. They had a team, bro, and they were proud of us. Things started happening there, and I don't know if we had anything to do with it, but I know it happened at the same time.

We played the game the right way. We had everything,

As the "Bad Boys" we beat people's ass.

just everything. To win in the NBA during that time period, when the league was at its all-out best, you had to be damn good. We were. This was the best time for the NBA, with Magic and Larry Bird leading the way. We were right there; we won two titles in a row, something the Celtics didn't do.

We played hard, physical basketball—that became our trademark as the "Bad Boys." We beat people's ass, as simple as

that. But we could finesse people too. We could beat you with any tactic there was, and nothing we did was cheap.

David Stern and other people around the league think I'm a threat to the game because I play dirty, but the problem isn't me. I'm doing the same things we did with the Pistons back then, only it's not accepted now like it used to be. The NBA decided to promote us as the "Bad Boys," and now six or seven years later it's not cool to play like that. The difference isn't me, it's the league. They've discouraged the kind of badass basketball that we played because they think it's dirty. It isn't—it's good basketball, and **THE GAME WOULD BE BETTER IF THESE YOUNG GUYS COULD BE CONVINCED TO PUT THEIR BALLS ON THE LINE** like we did back then. They're all too worried about dunks and scoring to play that style, though.

We would target players to stop on the other team. It was almost like a football mentality. Our strength was intimidating guys, taking them out of their game so we could run the game the way we wanted it to be run. We were smart about it too. We knew we weren't going to stop Michael Jordan; we let Michael score his 40 and shut down Scottie Pippen and everybody else. We'd target Pippen and make sure Michael didn't have much help. We'd say, **"GO AHEAD, BRO. IF YOU'RE GOOD ENOUGH TO BEAT US BY YOURSELF, IT'S ALL YOURS."** Sometimes he was good enough, but we usually wore them down. The only time the Bulls beat us in the playoffs—out of four series—was in 1991, when they beat us in four straight and ended up winning the first of three straight titles.

There was a feeling out there that we tried to hurt people, but we never did. We were playing basketball. Believe me, if we had wanted to hurt somebody, we could have done it easily. We could have had players going to the hospital all fucking night with the guys we had on our team. We were not only big enough and tough enough, but we knew how to hurt people. *There was some street-tough shit on that roster.*

Everybody hated Laimbeer, though. He loved that role. Anyone who has ever played the game would want a guy like Laimbeer on their team. He didn't have a fear in the world. He didn't care who the fuck it was he was knocking down. He didn't care if you were black or white, somebody or nobody. He was going to knock the shit out of your ass, and then he was going to finish it up by spitting on you and cussing your ass out. He was something else, bro, and everybody in the league hated his ass for it.

Laimbeer would stomp on a guy and make him feel like shit. Then the next time he'd play that guy, we'd be standing out there for the tip-off and we'd hear Laimbeer telling the guy, **"REMEMBER what I did to your ass last time? Well, GET READY, because I'm about to do the same thing all over again."**

His problem was he never tried to hide anything. He was always spotted, doing shit in the wide open. Everybody in the league knew what he was going to do, but everybody in the league also knew there was a guy on their own team trying to do the same thing, who just wasn't good enough. Laimbeer played the white-men-can't-jump role perfectly, but he could play the game. He was one of the best-shooting centers in basketball, and he hit the big shot for us all the time. He was more than a thug, but that's what he'll be remembered for.

Robert Parish will be remembered for scoring points and being part of that Celtics frontcourt, with Larry Bird and Kevin McHale, but **Robert Parish did just as much shit as Laimbeer did.** Parish was just smarter about it. He did it when nobody was looking, but Laimbeer didn't give a shit if anybody was looking. He was more open about it, so the NBA kept watching him and sitting on him.

Laimbeer was in his own world on the court. He was a cool guy to us off the court, but he still had that look in his eyes. *People would come up to him and ask for his autograph, and he'd look down at them and say,* **"FUCK OFF"** That's the way he was. That was Bill Laimbeer.

We lived for the playoffs in those years. We started out with a plan at the beginning of every year, and we weren't going to accept anything less than a trip to the Finals. We won two in a row after losing in 1988, and except for a bad call on Laimbeer—he supposedly fouled Kareem Abdul-Jabbar in the last minute of Game 7 against the Lakers in 1988—we would have won three titles in a row, just like the Bulls did to start the 1990s.

You can't play the playoffs at the same speed as the regular season. Just can't be done, bro. Everything tightens up in the playoffs, and the physical teams have a huge edge. We were built for the playoffs with that front line of me, Adrian Dantley, Laimbeer, and Mahorn.

That first year, 1988, we set out to beat the Celtics in the Eastern Conference Finals. We'd lost to them in seven games in the Eastern Conference Finals my rookie year, and we took so much shit in Boston Garden during that series that **we came to camp the next year with one thought: BEAT BOSTON.**

It almost didn't matter what we got after that, just so we got them.

We did too. We beat them in six games to pretty much end their run of dominance in the Eastern Conference. The next two years it was Chicago and a whole new set of problems for us to overcome.

As good as those Celtics teams were, the main thing everyone will remember in twenty years is Larry Bird. I think I got to know Larry Bird's game as well as or better than anybody in the league during those years, and he was a challenge.

WHENEVER BIRD COMES UP, RACE COMES UP. White people liked to see him hanging with the black dudes, because he was one of the only guys who could do it at the highest level. I made the mistake of bringing up race after the seventh game of the Eastern Conference Finals in my rookie year. I'll get more into this later, when I talk about race, but here's the basics: After the Celtics beat us, everyone was talking about Bird and I said I thought he was overrated because he was white. I brought it up first, but Isiah agreed and the whole thing just exploded. Isiah and Larry had this little press conference in Boston after that series. They sat up there and Isiah told everyone it was a big misunderstanding. He said all the Pistons had the greatest respect for Larry, which was true. Bird just kind of sat there and accepted the apology. I started the thing, and then I went home to the Riches in Oklahoma to read my hate mail.

The next year, again in the Eastern Conference Finals, I was on Bird the whole series. There were guys I could intimidate with my eyes or by getting in their ass and not letting them move, but Bird wasn't one of them. Taking him on was like playing a computer game. You had to try to get into his mind and anticipate what he was going to do next. That was the hardest part, because he was always thinking way ahead of everybody on the floor.

The only thing to do was get used to him. Watch tapes, watch him closely on the floor, and try to beat him to the spot. We played them enough that I started to get used to him, but it was never comfortable.

Even though he wasn't fast and he didn't go much for fancy dunks or anything like that, ***Bird was one of the few white guys who could play what people call the "Black Game."*** I respected Larry. I respected anybody who could go out and kick my ass, and he did it often enough. I would respect him as long as the game was on, but afterward? No way. I'd walk off the floor thinking, **I've got to go kick his ass next time.**

41

I don't think Larry respected me at the beginning. He talked shit his whole career, but I remember him during that first Eastern Conference Finals. He was talking so much, it was like everybody got used to it. He was mostly asking everybody who was guarding him. He'd be looking around like he couldn't see me standing there, and he'd ask guys on both teams, **"WHO'S GUARDING ME?"** Sometimes he'd ask me.

Later, Larry respected me. He had to, bro. I started stopping him just about every time he had the ball. He would never say anything to me, then. He kept his mouth shut then, bro. He would never give me the satisfaction of knowing I was getting the best of him—just like I never let him know when he was getting the best of me.

Our goal the year we beat the Celtics was reached: We were in the Finals. After that we didn't have a plan. Back then we always thought the Eastern Conference was the tough part. We'd have a tough series against Washington or Chicago, then have to face the Celtics. The Lakers had it easier getting to the Finals, and they were waiting for us.

It was almost like we went into that series saying, "Here you go. **We're going to give you this series, and next year we're going to come back here and kick your ass."** It was hard to win a Finals when you hadn't been there before; the intensity went up and up.

The sad thing is, we could have won that series in '87. We were up by three points with forty seconds to go in Game 7, and Kareem missed a shot. It came right down to me and we were ready to run out the clock. Then the whistle. Foul on Laimbeer.

Laimbeer was two feet away from Kareem. There was no way, bro. Kareem hit two free throws, we missed a shot, and they hit one to win it. That was it. They were running all over the place hugging each other and we were motherfuckin' the referees and throwing shit around the locker room.

I try not to get into the one-on-one battles on the court.

Some guys live for that, the back and forth firing in some-body's face, but that's not for me. I'm not going to try to get you back, so what's it matter? I'm just not going to let you score. I'll give you a break when you come back on defense.

A lot of players back then started to think about me first and what they had to do second. Scottie Pippen was that way. I would get into their minds, and before the game they'd be thinking, *Oh, fuck, I might only get ten or twelve points this game.* I'd go out of the game, and when I came back in, I always made sure to look the guy right in the eyes. I could see the look on their faces. It said, **Oh, shit, here comes this crazy son of a bitch again.**

They could see the expression on my face and my body movements, and they didn't want to come into contact with me at all. They wanted nothing to do with me. **I WAS TOO DIFFERENT, *TOO WEIRD.*** You could just see it.

One time Darrell Walker of the Washington Bullets got so pissed off at me that he tried to kick me, then he tried to spit on me. I had given him a little shot here and there, and he decided he was going to retaliate that way. I was eating this up. This was what I lived for. His spit missed me, though, that was the only bad part. I wanted him to hit me.

Right there on the court I told him, **"If you're going to spit at me, make sure you hit me in the face. Don't be wasting my time."**

I don't care—spit on me, yell at me, kick me. Whatever you do to me is going to pump me up more. The worse you do, the more I like it. **I LOVED GOING OUT THERE AND SHUTTING DOWN THE PRETTY BOYS OF THE NBA.** I shut down just about everybody who thought they were a badass—Clyde Drexler, Dominique Wilkins, Bird, Pippen. I love to see the smooth, styling players get taken out of their game. I don't give a shit out there. I run around and throw my body on the floor and do whatever the team needs.

I used to look at the guy I was guarding and think, *Fuck this. I just decided something:* **YOU AIN'T GET-TING SHIT.** They might come away with their 20 points or so, but the deal was, I was always there at the end to stop them from getting the game-winner. That's what I was known for. I might get in trouble early in a game for being too aggressive, but what I wanted was this: to set a tone for the rest of the game, so when it came down to that last-second shot, they were thinking about me instead of their job.

The Eastern Conference was a war, and it didn't get any easier when Boston started to fade out. Chicago was coming on at the same time, so we had another badass team to beat to get to the Finals.

Chicago was a mental thing. **TRYING TO BEAT JORDAN, JUST THINKING ABOUT IT, COULD WEAR YOU OUT.** We beat them in six games to go to the Finals in 1988—against the Lakers again.

We swept the Lakers. We just kicked their ass. We were in the second stage of our goal, and we weren't going to go in and mess around this time. Just like we had a plan to beat the Celtics after we lost in the Eastern Conference Finals my rookie year, we had a plan to beat the Lakers. We had that title won in training camp of that year.

WINNING *was the greatest, bro.* When we won that first title, it was hard to describe what I felt for that team. I already knew Chuck Daly was the greatest, but the way that team came together was unbelievable. We didn't always like each other off the court, but on the court everything was cool. We were able to put it all aside and play the game the way it had to be played. You might have a problem with a guy on Tuesday morning, but on Tuesday night, in the third quarter of a close game, that guy was your best friend.

If you want to know why the teams in San Antonio couldn't do the same thing, your answer's right there.

The Spurs couldn't put everything aside and just play the damn game.

They didn't know how to do that. We had a big parade and all that after we won the title, and the city was crazy. If we had won in San Antonio, I wouldn't have gone to the parade. I would have just got on my Harley and disappeared after the last game. I didn't feel enough of a part of that team to celebrate. Those things are for the people of the city.

I think the Portland team we played to win our second championship was another team that was never ready to win. They just went into that series like they didn't know they had to win. They went in without knowing it was now or never. We got lucky in Detroit, because we were good enough to come back and make up for losing to the Lakers. These guys from Portland didn't realize they were playing a team that was a lot hungrier.

The Trail Blazers got there twice, in 1990 and '92, and came away with nothing. You accomplished something getting there, bro, but you've got to come away with something.

I. I was on that Portland team, we would have won at least one of those series. With that kind of talent—Clyde Drexler, Jerome Kersey, Kevin Duckworth, Buck Williams— there's no way in hell we would have lost two in a row. With me they would have known how to win. They didn't know the mind game. They didn't have any kind of plan. Their only plan was, *"We lost. We got to get back there." That was their idea of a plan.*

They had athletes and physical tools, but that's not what the game's all about once you get to the Finals. Once you get there, it's all about which team has its mind right.

I was glad to see Drexler get his ring with Houston in 1995. I think he persevered through all the bullshit in Portland, then got an opening and walked through it in Houston. He showed some toughness people wondered whether he had.

That series against the Blazers wasn't very memorable.

There aren't many things that stick with me, except something Clyde said after Game 2. I bet as soon as he said it, he wished he could have had it back.

Portland won the second game in Detroit, and Clyde popped off after it. **"WE'RE NOT COMING BACK TO DETROIT,"** he said.

Bro, Clyde was right on. We didn't come back to Detroit. **We swept them three games in Portland and had ourselves another ring.**

The year we won our second title was the year I won my first Defensive Player of the Year award. They presented me with the trophy at a banquet, and when they gave it to me I cried. I couldn't believe this was me. To me, that was a sign that I had made it all the way. All the way from nowhere. I had set out to play defense and rebound, and I was recognized as the best defensive player in the NBA. *As I stood up there receiving the award, I thought about how far I'd come*

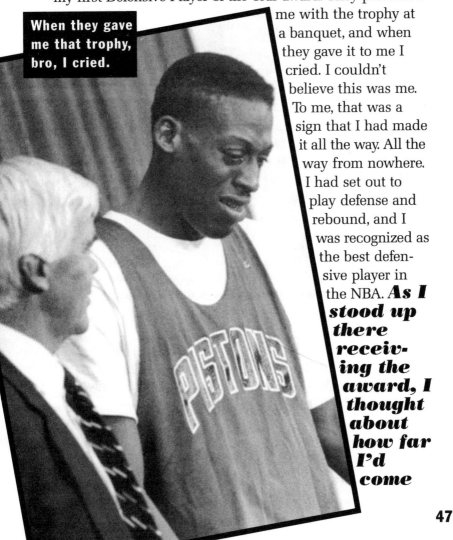

When they gave me that trophy, bro, I cried.

and how many people helped me get there. When all that comes rushing back at me, I can't hold it in.

The difference between Durant, Oklahoma, and the NBA is about as big as you could ever guess. It's like going from a closet into a mansion, and I wasn't ready for all of it. Some of the stuff off the court I just had to experience for myself; nobody was going to be able to tell me what to do or what not to do. I had to find my own way and make my own mistakes.

I did all right with the girls in college, but this was a different league, bro. The women were everywhere, and it was like there were no rules. Other players would tell me where to go in certain cities and where not to go, and sometimes there would be guys whispering in my ear, saying, "Don't do this, Dennis. Be careful." The thing was, **I didn't know there were that many people out there trying to take advantage of someone just because he's got a little power and a little money.**

It wasn't just women trying to take advantage of me either. Sometimes I'd go to a club or a party and someone would come up to me and hand me some marijuana or try to get me to do some cocaine. A bunch of times people would come up to me and hand me a little piece of paper and tell me to put it on my tongue. I remember the first time that happened, I asked someone what the fuck it was. He said, "You don't know? **THAT'S ACID, BRO.**"

I threw all that shit away. I guess people thought because I looked different and acted wild that I must do drugs. They still think that way, even though everybody who knows me knows I'm the last guy who's going to start doing drugs. **I'VE GOT ENOUGH PROBLEMS KEEPING MYSELF UNDER CONTROL WITHOUT PUTTING SOME SHIT IN MY BODY**

THAT'S SUPPOSED TO MAKE ME WILD. I do all right on that without any help.

It's the same idea as people buying you a drink when you're in a bar. They just want to be able to tell their friends they bought Dennis Rodman a drink, and then we drank together. That happens all the time, and it's no big deal.

On our one trip to Sacramento in my rookie year, I met a model named Annie Bakes in a bar after the game. This was the second year the Kings were in Sacramento, and the city wasn't anybody's favorite stop. There wasn't much of anything to do, and the hotel was kind of out of the way. But there were three bars right near the hotel where all the players—and, of course, all the women—used to hang out after games.

I was still naive about this NBA stuff. I was right out of Oklahoma, and I was still pretty innocent. Annie and I got along great. We hung out, slept together—the whole thing. We saw each other a few times after that, and the next year she was pregnant. My daughter, Alexis, was born on September 28, 1988.

See, she looks just like me.

Annie and I didn't get married because I didn't think it would work out. It just wasn't right. I loved my daughter and tried to see her as much as I could, but I didn't think I could go through with the marriage.

I think marriage and athletes is a bad combination. There are too many diversions for an athlete to make a marriage work. I'm not saying all athletes' marriages are bad, because there are a lot of guys who are faithful and happy. Most of the time, though, the circumstances don't allow you to be married and happy because you haven't fulfilled all your fantasies. **THE DOORS FLY OPEN WHEN YOU'RE A PROFESSIONAL ATHLETE.**

Everybody wants a piece of you. Women are everywhere, just asking to be taken home and fucked. It's very difficult for a human being to sit there in a room with all this going on and not give in to the temptation. If you're sitting at home with your wife, you know there's something waiting just outside that door, and you can't help but think about it. It takes a strong man and a strong woman to make it work.

But we did get married, eventually. We were in Lake Tahoe in September of 1992. This was just before training camp opened in my last year with the Pistons. We were at a hotel in Tahoe—Alexis, Annie, and me—and Alexis kept asking, *"Daddy, when are you going to marry Mommy? Daddy, will you please marry Mommy?"*

What could I say? My daughter's almost four years old, and she's begging me to marry her mother. It's hard to keep saying, "No. No. No. No."

So we got married. Right there, in Tahoe. Eighty-two days later it was over.

We never should have gotten married. We weren't right for each other. Of the eighty-two days we were married, we were together for about a month. She'd live with me in Detroit for a couple weeks, then something would happen and I'd send her and Alexis home to Sacramento for a couple weeks, then they'd come back. We repeated that a few times.

It was not a marriage like most people think of marriage. We were married for the child, and I should have known that wasn't going to work out in the long run. We had our own relationships outside the marriage. I can't say too much about that because I was as much at fault as Annie was.

I'll put it this way: **I think Annie did her share of window-climbing, and I did my share of door-cracking.** I think we both did our share of sneaking out. I wasn't hiding anything from her; she knew what was going on, and so did I. I don't want to go any farther with it than that, because we had no business being married in the first place.

I should have figured from the start that my marriage wouldn't work, because I married for the wrong reasons. I got married for the good of my child. Part of me thought everything could be all right if I went ahead and did this. I thought maybe everything could work out. My daughter is beautiful, and I love her, but it didn't do her any good to have us married for that short time. I should have known better.

We were back and forth the whole time. I felt Annie was trying to turn my daughter against me by talking me down in front of her. I thought the baby was being taught to have a bad outlook on her father, and I couldn't say anything because I knew it wouldn't do any good. All kids take their mother's side, that's just human nature. It got worse after we were divorced—what could I do then? She had the baby, and I was left out in the cold.

It was doomed from the start, and I'm sorry for both of us. You do crazy things for the kids you love, and that was probably the craziest thing I did. We already had our own lives, so it was hard to try to put them together and make them work.

The divorce came during the season, and it helped to make that whole season a mess. It was already bad

51

because Chuck Daly was gone and the team was starting to fall apart. **I just couldn't take any MORE SHIT.** It was one of the hardest years for me, because everything seemed to hit me at once. I wasn't seeing my daughter as much as I wanted. Annie was back in Sacramento, and I was traveling around with a basketball team that didn't seem to care anymore.

The things Annie and I went through were typical things that divorced people go through all the time.

She was doing what I thought were crazy things: She refused to let me see Alexis; she said she was going to leave and go to Europe and never let me see my daughter.

Even when I did get to see Alexis, it was hard. Things were so strained between me and Annie that it was tough for us to be together, even when it was for Alexis. That year, for the first time, I couldn't even escape my problems through basketball.

A lot of people back then wanted to say I self-destructed because of Annie, but that's wrong. There's no way in hell—any problems I had after our relationship ended had to do with Alexis and not Annie. I wouldn't let a woman destroy my life or distract me from what I'm doing. Annie could go off and marry another man and it wouldn't matter to me, as long as I still got to be with my daughter.

Everything that happened that last year in Detroit—all the depression I was feeling, all the supposedly self-destructive things I did—were about basketball.

I was rebelling against a lot of stuff that went on after they broke up our championship team. I would never turn my back on people who helped me, and what I was doing then was turning my back on people who were destroying that franchise, such as Billy McKinney, who took over as general manager after Jack McCloskey left.

McKinney had a lot to do with Chuck Daly leaving. **WHEN DALY LEFT, I THINK HE TOOK SOME OF ME WITH HIM.** I couldn't take it when they fired him. I respect Chuck Daly more than anyone in the league, and it killed me to have to play the last year there without him. The way he was treated his last three years there wasn't right. He had a one-year contract every year, even when we were winning back-to-back titles. His money wasn't even guaranteed. I saw how this business works by watching how they treated Chuck Daly.

McKinney and the other people in Detroit did a lot of terrible things to Chuck Daly that nobody will ever know about. I know, because I was there for seven years, but I don't think it's my place to say anything.

Daly and I used to talk all the time when he was coach, but I almost never said a word to Ron Rothstein, who took over for Daly. It was a messed-up year, and as the season went along it got nothing but worse.

Our great team just vanished. Rich Mahorn was gone after the 1988–89 season. James Edwards and Vinnie Johnson left after the 1990–91 season. John Salley was traded after the 1991–92 season. Laimbeer was still around, but he wasn't playing much. The only guys who were still there were Isiah, Joe Dumars, and me. I could see it coming, though: I was next.

McCloskey, the man who had drafted me, was gone. Even the trainer was gone. Everybody was either gone or leaving, and the thing was, they didn't have any players to replace the guys who left.

I had contract problems too. I had signed a six-year, $10 million contract before the 1990–91 season, and since then I'd become an All-Star and the league's best rebounder, while the salaries had skyrocketed for the newer players. Management told me they understood the situation and would take care of me, but they went back on that when things went bad during that awful season.

I decided right then **this was a COLD-HEARTED BUSINESS.** With everything else going on in my life, all I was asking was for somebody to appreciate what I'd done and pay me in line with the production. I realized there was no loyalty, no commitment, no anything. I would have stayed in Detroit my whole career if the others had stayed too. Because that didn't happen, I wanted out. **I felt I got left behind in a foxhole.**

For the first time I felt more like a commodity than a person. Chuck Daly wouldn't have let it happen like that, but the new people didn't know how to take me. Story of my life, when it comes to management types. I got the feeling I had to do what they said or I'd be gone.

I took a stand. I told them the nature of the business was bullshit, and I asked for a trade.

My reward for that was **a trip to San Antonio and two more years of lies.**

Toward the end of that final season in Detroit, **I ended up in my pickup in the parking lot of The Palace, staring at the rifle and listening to Pearl Jam.**

My marriage was pretty much a fatal attraction from the beginning, not because Annie is violent—she's not—but because it wasn't right from the start. Then, like all divorces, it seems like all this evilness comes out and makes it harder still. The child should be the main thing, but all of a sudden the money takes over and becomes the most important thing.

I won't deny that the marriage changed me. It changed the way I looked at people, and it changed the way I decided whether to trust someone. It changed the way I think about women and relationships. **It put a force field around my whole life,** and it made me distrust everything about this game and the life it provides for you.

I think **I GOT USED** in the marriage. I think **I GOT TRICKED** into marriage. I think **IT WAS A SETUP** from the start. I got used within the system. There's a woman who supposedly loves you, and then all of a sudden she turns around and tries to take every dime you've got. Why? Because it belongs to her all of a sudden, after eighty-two days of marriage? No, it does not.

Lord knows, any man who doesn't take care of his child is stupid. I give her $10,000 a month. Is that all going to my child? No. It's all right to provide the woman with a comfortable living for a short period of time, then after a while, the woman has to take responsibility and stand on her own two feet. When you start taking care of the child and taking care of the woman—for life—that's another story. She shouldn't have what the man has, because the man made it where he is without her.

I've got a reward out of my relationship with Annie, and that's a beautiful little girl. I don't see her as much as I would like, I admit that, but there have been things that have made it hard—things I have no control over.

I've got this beautiful daughter, and sometimes I feel like I just pay rent.

One of my favorite Pearl Jam songs is called "Daughter," and one of the lines in it is a daughter telling her father, **"DON'T CALL ME DAUGHTER."** That song really hits me, because I could write a song about me and my father where I would say, ***"Don't call me son."*** When I listen to that song, I think about Alexis every time. I'm afraid it's a cycle, and ***I'm afraid that someday Alexis is going to say the same thing to me.***

four

Sports Slave

The High-Stakes World of Selling Out

I'm not like the other guys in the NBA. I'm different, and it goes beyond the way I look and the things I do off the court. Here's the main difference: **I speak my mind. Everybody else is going to do what they're told because they're the NBA Kids. They have to say something that won't burn their daddy's feet, and that daddy is Commissioner David Stern.**

I don't care if I burn those feet. You're nothing as a man if you can't speak from the heart. There are people in this league who allow themselves to be controlled by the image the league wants to project. They're the ones who are scared they might say the wrong thing and get punished for it.

That's not me. I say what I feel in my heart and in my mind.

The NBA image of a man is the one they put out on the

commercials, with guys smiling and waving to the crowd. All that happy horseshit. They want everyone to be Grant Hill—a guy from Duke with all the flashy moves. Grant Hill can play, I've got no problem with him, but isn't there room for some other kind of player out there? Some other kind of *man*?

I DON'T FIT INTO THE MOLD OF THE NBA MAN, AND I THINK I'VE BEEN PUNISHED FINANCIALLY FOR IT. Nobody wants to hear an athlete cry and whine about the money he makes, but respect comes in different forms in different professions.

Everybody likes to be appreciated for what they can do. Kids like to be complimented for what they do in school, cabdrivers like to be appreciated with good tips, and basketball players like to be paid in line with their production on the court. Everybody competes in this league—for rebounds, for wins, for women, for money. I know what other players at my position make, and they know what I make. It may be childish, but we compare.

I make $2.5 million a year. Nobody is going to feel sorry for me because of that, and nobody should. But the people also need to understand the kind of money that's available out there. The NBA is a billion-dollar business. They're filling arenas all over the place. Walk into any mall in any city in the United States and you'll see at least three stores selling licensed NBA jerseys, shorts, sweatpants, baseball caps. The money is there for some people, but for others the door is closed. I make a lot of money, but when you look at my performance, my contribution, then you see I'm way in the back of the NBA's money train.

I think I should be paid as one of the top three or four power forwards in the league. **DERRICK COLEMAN OF THE PHILADELPHIA 76ERS MAKES MORE THAN $7 MILLION A YEAR, AND I THINK I'M BETTER THAN DERRICK COLEMAN.** The only thing he does better than Dennis Rodman is score points. The problem is, most people would think that statement is foolish, because most people think scoring points is the only way you win games. I think my career shows that I've come up with a different way, and it's a better way than the one Derrick Coleman uses. I rebound and I play defense, and those two things help me make the people around me better players. David Robinson is a perfect example of that; he won a scoring title and an MVP award in the two years he played with me in San Antonio. In Detroit, Bill Laimbeer was able to stay outside and hit big shots because Chuck Daly knew I would be inside taking care of the boards. Derrick Coleman scores, and that's about it. **Who benefits from what he does on the floor? Only Derrick Coleman.**

Also, Derrick Coleman does not have two championship rings, and I do.

Derrick Coleman? I think I'm better than him.

Derrick Coleman does not bring people to the building, and I do.

Attendance in San Antonio was second in the NBA my first year there. They moved into the Alamodome that year, so they had more seats to sell—and my presence helped the team sell them. That's part of the reason they got me. We averaged 22,053 fans a game my first year there, and the only other team to average more than 20,000 was the Charlotte Hornets, who averaged more than 23,000.

The Spurs had never been as far as the Western Conference Finals until I got there. In 1994–95 we had the league's best record and went to the conference finals. David Robinson won the Most Valuable Player award, largely because I was there to take some of the rebounding pressure off him.

I bring something to the people. ***Derrick Coleman doesn't. Chris Dudley doesn't,*** and the Portland Trail Blazers are paying him $6 million a year. ***Anthony Mason doesn't*** do what I do, and the New York Knicks signed him for more than $4 million a year. To me none of this computes.

I've learned something through all the years of diving for loose balls and coming down with the flamboyant rebound: People want excitement, enjoyment, and a winning team. They also want something different. From the first time I colored my hair, I knew that. I walked out onto the court in San Antonio with bleach-blond hair, and right away I saw how much those **PEOPLE LOVED WHAT DENNIS RODMAN WAS GIVING THEM.** The excitement was right there, right now. That's what this game is all about, and all I ask is that somebody see it and appreciate it. It's no different than a waitress wanting to be acknowledged when people keep coming back to her restaurant because her service is so good.

I feel **I've been used** for the past four or five years to provide entertainment to the fans and money to the league owners. They used me for marketing in San Antonio, because they knew I was popular with the fans. Others teams did the same thing. When we were on the road, you could watch the commercials for the other team and hear them telling people, "Come out and watch Dennis Rodman and the San Antonio Spurs." Same thing on the radio.

They didn't have a problem with me being *WILD AND CRAZY* when it came time to fill the arenas.

But every time it was my turn—when it was time for somebody to step forward and say, "Okay, let's take care of Dennis Rodman and give him the security he needs"—I was told there was nothing left.

Before the 1990–91 season I signed a six-year contract worth $10 million—not bad money for a guy who traveled such a bizarre road to the NBA. I was coming off my first NBA Defensive Player of the Year award, and I played in my first All-Star Game. I was on a roll, and the Pistons were on a roll. We'd just won our second straight NBA championship in Detroit, and I was thinking I could stay there for the rest of my career.

Then the salaries went crazy the next couple of years, and I just kept getting better and better. I was second in the league in rebounding in 1990–91 and won another Defensive Player of the Year award. The next year I led the league in rebounding with 18.7 boards a game—the highest average in the NBA in twenty years.

The contract I signed didn't look so good then.

The Pistons management agreed with this. They said they would take care of me, but they didn't. That's why I was traded in the first place. They said they understood my situation, but I guess understanding it and doing something about it are two different things.

The same thing happened twice in San Antonio, in remarkably similar ways. Spurs general manager Bob Bass told me they couldn't do anything right away, but they assured me they would redo the contract as soon as the season ended. I was led to believe the contract renegotiation was part of the package when I was traded for Sean Elliott. I wouldn't have accepted the trade if I didn't think they were going to rip up my contract.

After that year ended, I'm all ready to see a two-year contract for about $14 million. Those were the numbers that were on the table. Instead, Bass and the coach, John Lucas, left. The new guys, mostly general manager Gregg Popovich, said they didn't know anything about it.

I GIVE MY *heart and soul* TO THIS
GAME, and just once I'd like to see someone give some of
theirs back to me. I give a lot of enjoyment to the people
who watch me play basketball. People who watch me play
go through the same emotions I do on the court. I look at
myself as one of the three top draws in the NBA. **If it's
not SHAQUILLE O'NEAL, and if it's not
MICHAEL JORDAN,** IT'S DENNIS RODMAN. And
those guys get paid way beyond anything I could hope to
get. If you want to talk total income—NBA salary plus
endorsements—Michael makes more than $35 million a
year, Shaq more than $25 million. I weigh in at $3 million
total.

I'm not even in the same universe with those guys when
it comes to pay. The system doesn't work for me; I work for
the system. The league gets what it wants, and the team
I'm playing for gets what it wants. Then there's me, *out
in the fucking cold.* When I try to speak up,
rationally, and explain how wrong it is, it's always the
same: Wait your turn.

They tell me they'd like to wait and see how I perform,
then they'll assess the situation. But **assess this: I
led the league in rebounding four
straight years and nothing changed.**
I brought money and recognition to the San Antonio Spurs
and nothing changed. What more could I do? After going
through it for so long, I hear only one voice, and it's saying, **"THE HELL WITH YOU, Dennis
Rodman.** Thanks a lot. Bye. We're going to screw you,
and we're going to continue to screw you."

All of this has to do with my personality. They don't
think I'm the right kind of **family man** or *role
model* or **LOCKER-ROOM LEADER.**

There's something in that I don't understand.
I thought all along I was a basketball player.

I thought that was the only thing that mattered. You
don't pay me to be a guardian angel. You don't pay me to
go to team picnics and hug everybody's wife and kiss

everybody's kids. You pay me to play this game. If I do that, it should be good enough.

With me it never is good enough. **I'M NOTHING MORE THAN A SPORTS SLAVE.** If it's going to be all about money, then I might as well play that game and try to get what I'm worth. We're all being used in this business, and some guys can sit back and take the trade-off—the NBA's money for their soul. Sorry, but I can't do it that way.

T he NBA wants everyone to be the same. They want the whole league to be filled with guys who never say anything controversial and never do anything they consider bad for the game.

They get away with it because **most of the players in the NBA are BRAINWASHED** to think that way. These guys were the top dogs in college, and they expect to be treated the same way when they get to the NBA. The whole world is just one long golden road.

I look at it through different eyes. There aren't many guys in the league who came from a background like mine. Not many NBA players went from being a janitor after high school, then to Cooke County Junior College and Southeastern Oklahoma. **When I was twenty years old, I was a janitor in the Dallas-Fort Worth Airport. When Shaquille O'Neal was twenty, he was making millions of dollars and publishing his autobiography.**

So many of these guys were practically household names when they were in high school. **Jason Kidd, Jamal Mashburn, Anfernee Hardaway—** they were known by basketball people across the country by the time they were high school juniors. They were groomed to play in the NBA from a young age. They've been after that one goal ever since they can remember, and there was always someone there to tell them they were going to make it. **Once a player like that gets to the NBA, he acts like it's something owed to him.**

For me this is a totally mind-boggling experience. My path wasn't golden—it wasn't even paved. I didn't really play basketball in high school, and the only people who knew about me when I was eighteen were my family and the police. It might not have been the ideal background, but it gave me another perspective. I know something other than basketball, and I know what can happen if basketball isn't here.

David Stern and the league would love it if I just went away. They'd give anything to have Dennis Rodman out of their hair, so they didn't have to worry about fining me or suspending me or whatever. They wouldn't have to worry about what I might be doing next to **tarnish the sacred image of the NBA.**

The incident I had with John Stockton in the second game of our first-round playoff series against the Utah Jazz in 1994 is a perfect example.

If you took a survey of all the players in the NBA, asking them who *the dirtiest guard in the NBA* is, who do you think they'd say? They'd probably say Stockton, but nobody outside the league would guess him.

JOHN STOCKTON GETS AWAY WITH ALL KINDS OF SHIT on the court. He throws elbows like you wouldn't believe. In that series he was playing his usual game, doing dirty shit away from the ball when the referees couldn't see him. Everyone gets tired of his act, and I decided to do something about it. When he came through the lane trying to run through a screen on offense, I stuck my hip out and sent him flying. It was blatant; I wasn't trying to hide anything.

The worst-kept secret in the NBA is the star system. Everybody knows it exists. It protects guys like Stockton, who do things on the court that only the guys who are out there could know. In the league's eyes certain people can do no wrong.

The league fined me $10,000 and suspended me for the next game, the third game of the series. We went on to get our asses kicked in that game, by a score of 105–72. **David Robinson did not show up for that**

game; he was there, and he played, but he didn't really show up. He had 16 points and 11 rebounds, *just another case of him coming up small in big games.*

The Stockton incident got me a meeting with David Stern. He called me into the office to discuss the situation before we flew to Utah for the third game. Stern and everybody else in the league thought I was playing dirty, and he wanted to make sure I knew he was setting out to clean up the league.

I sat down across from him and he said, "You're a great player without that stuff, Dennis. You don't have to play like that."

I told him the truth.

"I really didn't do anything that others guys don't do. It's just that I did it out in the open, where everybody could

65

see it. If you're going to complain to me and make me look like an asshole, why not complain to everybody else who does the same damned thing but doesn't get noticed for it?"

Maybe Stern doesn't even know what goes on out there. Maybe he doesn't know that **Karl Malone gets away with all kinds of elbows and hips when he's under the basket.** But even if Stern doesn't know about these things, I still don't think it's fair to pick out one person and make him out to be the dirtiest player in the league. If you're trying to clean up a mess, don't make me the example for the whole league.

I'M AN EASY TARGET. Too easy. They point to me as the bad guy, and the public accepts it. They've come to expect that Dennis Rodman is going to be the bad boy of the NBA. They wouldn't do that with John Stockton; it might change the way people think about him.

The NBA decides who's going to be the chosen ones. When Grant Hill came out of Duke, he was anointed immediately. The publicity machine was in motion. He had already won the Rookie of the Year award, he'd already made the All-Star team. The league decided what he was going to be before he even played a game in the NBA.

Grant Hill fit the image of the NBA man perfectly. He came from Duke, so he'd been exposed nationally a million times over. Everybody knew him. Everybody loved him. He had the right looks. His father—Calvin Hill—was a great pro football player. His mother is a big-time Washington lawyer. He was articulate and lived a clean life. And on the basketball court he was flashy with his dunks and scored a lot of points. It was so perfect for the NBA; they could hardly believe their luck.

I THOUGHT IT WAS PATHETIC. The league just decided that Grant Hill would go right to the top; he had the commercials, the endorsements, everything. It was decided when Michael Jordan was off playing baseball: Grant Hill would be the next god of basketball. He would

Bad As I Wanna Be

take the throne from Michael.

What I want to know is, **why didn't they just crawl up into his ass** with their fucking telescope and tell us what else was going to happen? Let us know the whole future, bro.

But a funny thing happened

Grant Hill: the next god of basketball? Pathetic.

to the NBA during Hill's rookie year. Here comes Jason Kidd of the Dallas Mavericks, playing his ass off. Kidd is a hell of a player, but he didn't have the perfect NBA pedigree. He'd had some trouble before the draft, when he supposedly ran from his car after he got into an accident on a freeway in Oakland, California. It was real early in the morning, and he was coming from a club. That made all the papers, so some NBA teams wondered if his character was good enough for the NBA. Dallas decided it was, **and Kidd ended up doing more to help his team than Grant Hill did.**

Kidd put the NBA in a spot. So what do they do? CO-ROOKIES OF THE YEAR. THAT WAS THEIR CHICKEN-SHIT SOLUTION.

I have a question: How can you have a co-Rookie of the Year? How can you do that? Were they both the exact same? Anybody who thinks that was a coincidence is dead wrong.

The same thing happened in the 1993 All-Star Game, when John Stockton and Karl Malone shared the MVP when the game was played in Utah. **THAT WAS JUST SO PRECIOUS.**

The league wants to project this clean image, and they'll do anything to protect it. That image is all well and good, but, damn—don't overwhelm people with it and make it like everybody has to be like that. Everybody is not like Grant Hill. It's fine that he is, but I'm not.

The best years of my career, so far, were spent in Detroit, playing for Chuck Daly. He didn't buy into the NBA's line about clean image. He let me, and everybody on the team, be a man. If you produced in practice and in games, you played. If you didn't, you sat. It didn't matter who you were or what you'd done.

In my second year I started taking minutes from Adrian Dantley. He had been in the league a long time, he'd been an All-Star—but I was bringing more to the team, so I played. Chuck Daly wasn't worried about my life outside the court, unless it affected my play on the court.

He wasn't going to structure my life for me. I didn't have to be a certain way. He just gave me the opportunity. And when opportunity arrives for Dennis Rodman, he's going to dive in headfirst. I will not take anything for granted, because I started at the bottom and worked my way up to get what I have.

There are people out there who would go to see me play basketball who wouldn't go to see Grant Hill. People enjoy watching me play.

They like me and the things I stand for. The real people I see in clubs and on the street, they like me. **THEY**

DON'T IDENTIFY WITH GRANT HILL.

I attract the grunge crowd, the Generation X types. They know what I'm all about. I'm probably not the favorite among the guys in the suits and ties, but the real people come up to me after games and say, "When I come to see you play, I can't believe some of the things you do."

I ask them, "Why do you come to see me play'"

Almost every time, they say the same thing: "Because it's *interesting*."

They know it's not your typical white-collar guy going out there doing something that millions of Americans wish they could do—dunk a basketball. **I COME WITH THREE HUNDRED AND SIXTY-FIVE DAYS' WORTH OF DIFFERENT EQUIP-MENT,** and people like that.

I think people all over the world would like that, too, but I never had any hope of playing for any of the Olympic teams. In the Barcelona Olympics "Dream Team with Dennis Rodman" was a pipe dream. I didn't really care about it, but there are times when I think it would be really cool if I could play in an Olympic team. It would be something I could look back on someday and be glad I did.

Most of all, I'd like to be able to show the world that **our country's athletes aren't all from the same cookie-cutter.** On the court I think I could be the perfect player on a team full of scorers. The Olympic teams are like a big version of the Bulls, and any of those teams could have used a down-and-dirty rebounder who didn't want the ball.

There was no way in hell it was going to happen in Barcelona, though. It's **THE SAME BULLSHIT I ALWAYS FACE:** basketball wasn't the primary concern. I think the people at USA Basketball were afraid I might take over the spotlight if they put me in there. I'd be a big distraction, just like always. I guess I have to learn to live with that.

They might as well have put BIG DISTRACTION' above my locker in San Antonio. It was practically my name. Every time something came up to throw the team off track, the problem was me being a big distraction. I was a distraction my first year there because of the Stockton incident in the playoffs. That was the same series Madonna showed up to create another big distraction.

My second year in San Antonio, I became a big distraction when I didn't join the huddle in the playoffs and when I took my shoes off on the bench. They made me look like I was out of control. They created the distraction by treating me like a two-year-old kid. I wouldn't have acted that way if they had committed to me.

Gregg Popovich was the big problem in San Antonio. We didn't get along from the beginning. He's Mr. Discipline, Mr. Straight, Mr. Conservative. It was his first general manager's job, and he wanted everyone to know how important he was. He had no idea how to take me.

Popovich gave me the same line Bass had. He told me to wait until after the season. I knew I was being lied to and led on, and it got to the point where I knew they were going to keep doing it. They were going to hold shit over my head the whole time I was there. **Whatever I did could and would be held against me.** It was like they were keeping a list.

The deal is, **I know I screwed up in San Antonio,** but I did things for a reason. People out there don't realize they treated me like crap. Another thing people don't realize is that I've been taking my shoes off for years. **I HATE TO WEAR SHOES, and if you saw my feet you'd know why.** They look like old tree branches, all gnarled and bent. I don't like to have them all cramped up in shoes any more than I have to.

Everyone got the team's version of everything. My version hasn't been told until now. I'll talk a *lot* more about the shoes and the huddle later, but the point here is: They promised one thing and delivered another. After two years I was sick of it. What was I supposed to do, break out another jar of Vaseline and say, **"OKAY, here you go: I'M BENDING OVER FOR YOU GUYS AGAIN"?**

I wouldn't do it, and they knew it. That's why they traded me to Chicago for next to nothing. I was going to sit out and hold on to my pride and stick to what I believe in. I wasn't going to go back for the third year in a row and subject myself to that crap they delivered to Dennis Rodman. I was ready to sit out the season.

I had two strikes on me, and then they wanted me to go back up to the plate again. They were saying, "Here, swing at this little pea. See if you can hit it. If you can hit it, you get a new contract." That's unfair, and it's crap.

The Spurs tried to tell me they didn't have any money, but if you don't have money how can you pay David Robinson $9 million a year and Sean Elliott $6 million a year? Where is that money coming from? All I want is a two-year deal that's going to help put my mind at ease.

I think a lot of NBA teams use the salary cap as an excuse. When a team wants to do something, it always seems to be able to do it. Larry Johnson is making $87 million over twelve years in Charlotte. That's almost enough money to buy a team. Down the road, Shaquille O'Neal is going to want $100 million, and he'll get it—all within the salary cap.

I look around, and **I see Chris Dudley, Derrick Coleman, Dale Davis, and Anthony Mason making huge money, and I see injustice. Who buys a ticket to see those guys play?** I don't think the league wants to see me get what I deserve. The less I get, the better for the league, because they think **I MIGHT SET A BAD PRECEDENT FOR PLAYERS COMING UP.** If I get what

I want, what's to stop younger players from speaking their minds?

This isn't about greed for me. I want to be paid so my daughter, Alexis, is taken care of for the rest of her life. I'm in a league that's supposed to do those things: provide for you now so you have something when your skills are gone. I'm not looking for anything fancy in this. I could go live in a one-bedroom apartment, and if my daughter is taken care of, I'll be all right. **If I get a new contract, the first thing I'm going to do is take $250,000 and put it in an account for Alexis.** She won't be able to touch it until she's eighteen, and then it can be used for college. By the time she's twenty-five, she can have it all. That's my motivation.

If a team made a commitment to me, I think I might be willing to play by the rules. I've come to the point in my career where *I COULD BE A GOOD LITTLE BOY, AT THE RIGHT PRICE.*

You use me? Great, now let me use you for a while. Give me $15 million for two years and you can use me. We'll be using each other,

Alexis has her dad's strong legs.

CAPITAL CITY FSC
MAY 22, 1994

because you'll be giving me security for the rest of my life. We'll both get what we want.

Think about it this way: If I can bring you $50 million, why not give me $15 million? If I can bring you $50 million the first year and $100 million the next year—and keep this game interesting for millions of Americans—why not give me $15 million for two years? If someone told you to spend $15 million to make $150 million, don't you think you'd do it?

It won't happen, of course. Not even close. I know that much going in. I've been one of the most productive guys in the league for the last four or five years, and I feel I've been used within the system with not enough in return.

If we're going to look at this as a business and not a sport, then let's look at my contribution to the Spurs franchise in those same terms. I gave that team national exposure. I gave them new life. I gave them acceptance in the NBA as well as around the world.

The television ratings for Spurs games my last year showed that I'm a big draw in this league. The highest-rated playoff game, not counting the finals, was the fifth game of the Western Conference Finals between us and the Rockets. With all the crap that was going on with me in those playoffs, **do you think people were tuning in to see whether David Robinson could finally handle Hakeem Olajuwon? I don't think so.** I think people were tuning in to see what I was going to do next.

In the nine years I've been in the NBA, rookies have gotten a hell of a lot more valuable, even though the talent level, in my opinion, has gotten worse. It used to be that rookies had to earn their time on the court—and their money.

When the rookies' salaries started going crazy, the top guys got contracts like the one Larry Johnson got—$87 million over twelve years. Rookies started taking up all this salary-cap money, and it meant that a lot of players who had worked their asses off to make this the most prominent game in the world got brushed aside.

It pisses me off when they give a guy like Glenn Robinson $9 million a year when he doesn't understand the first thing about winning in the NBA. They see that he can score, and that's enough. The Milwaukee Bucks picked Robinson with the first pick of the 1994 draft, and I can just see them sitting at the table after the contract was signed. I picture someone saying, "Okay, Glenn, go out there and score some points."

The Bucks have the right to give Robinson whatever they want, but **I don't think they'll ever win a championship with that philosophy.** They'll give that kind of money to a guy who has shown one thing—that he can score in college—but nobody will give it to a guy who can control a game, make other players better, and bring fans to the arena. Why not pay that guy?

The rookie salary cap was the best thing to come out of the new contract between the players and the league. It was about time somebody did something to correct that crazy system.

When I talk about money, I always get hit with the same question. "Well," somebody says, **"are you going to show up for practice?"**

The perception out there, one created by the Spurs, is that I don't show up for practice. **I SHOW UP FOR PRACTICE.** I missed one practice during my last year in San Antonio, and I missed it because I didn't feel well. They didn't buy that reason, so they made a big deal out of it. When another guy says he doesn't feel well, they tell him to get some rest and take care of himself.

When John Lucas was my coach in San Antonio, he used to say, "Dennis isn't a problem. Sometimes he's a couple minutes late to practice, but all we do is shoot at the beginning of practice. Dennis doesn't shoot, anyway, so what's the problem?"

Another thing I hear is: "Are you going to be in the huddle?"

This whole huddle thing really **PISSES ME OFF.**

I'm in the huddle. If you look at every game film, I'm in the huddle. If you look at every team in the league, how many guys who are in the huddle are looking at people in the damn stadium? Watch a game and you'll see a lot of players—not just me—looking around the arena, wondering what they can get after the game. I bet you'll see more of that than guys staring at the coach.

It comes down to this: None of that small stuff matters. If I don't deserve the money, why don't I deserve it? Can David Robinson sit up there and say, "I deserve $8 million, even though I have never won a championship"?

If you take a poll about David Robinson around the league, what kind of response would you get?

Is he a good citizen? Yes.

Is he a good basketball player? Yes.

CAN HE WIN THE BIG ONE? NO.

CAN DENNIS RODMAN WIN THE BIG ONE? YES.

So you tell me, should I get paid or not?

David Robinson is a great player. He won the scoring title my first year in San Antonio, and he won the MVP in my second year. The deal is, though, he has to accept one fact: If you're going to be the MVP of the league, you've got to go out there and **prove it in the postseason. Hakeem Olajuwon did that. David Robinson didn't.**

I don't look at myself as an MVP. I'm not competing with David Robinson or Michael Jordan for the spotlight. I'm part of a unit. I'm where nobody wants to be. **I do the dirty work.** I take the flack. I take the pressure off my other teammates. It's what I love to do, and I wish somebody would see the value of it.

75

The NBA believes if you play for a team and get paid by a team, you're the property of that team for twenty-four hours a day. **They want to know what you eat, where you sleep, who you're sleeping with.** This might not be a problem for most players, but it is for me. The league has this fascination with me and my off-court activities.

Why should I let them know what I'm doing with my time? My job is to do what I do best, to go to practice and play in the games. After practice it's my life. They don't control me after I leave that building. It's not their business what I do after I leave that building.

I'll say it again: **YOU PAY ME TO PLAY BASKETBALL.** Just because you pay me, I don't give you the right to keep an eye on me twenty-four hours a day. The job of management is to provide what that city needs—a winner. They step over the line when they think they have to have twenty-four-hour surveillance on a player because he doesn't go home to a wife and three kids.

For years the league has thought I've been on drugs. It's the only way they can explain me, I guess. They don't realize I would have burned out a long time ago if that was true. It wouldn't have been a big secret.

In 1989, when I was with the Pistons, **the NBA hired someone to follow me around.** They wanted to know what the fuck was going on with me, so they put someone on me. This might be the perfect example of what I mean when I call myself a sports slave. Not even my private life was private.

Chuck Daly came up to me one day after practice and said, "The league's following you, Dennis." They had a private investigator out trying to figure out what I was doing away from the building. I never met the guy or saw the guy, and I didn't really give a shit. Nobody came up to me and said, **"HI, I'M A PRIVATE INVESTIGATOR for the NBA."** I don't think they operate like that.

I'd like to know whether that was the only time that was done to me. I think there's a good chance it happened while I was in San Antonio too.

One thing they might find out would surprise a lot of people. How many people in the NBA will come in before a game, work out, go out and play forty minutes, and then come back in after the game and work out again for another hour and a half? How many people in the league do you think do that?

I only know of one: Dennis Rodman.

I go into the weight room before a game and loosen up with some light weights. I like to feel strong when I go out on the floor, but I don't want to be bulky and stiff. I might warm up my legs on the stair machine or the stationary bicycle. I listen to Pearl Jam and get my mind right.

After the game I'll lift heavier weights. I find if I lift after the game, I have a longer recovery time than if I come in the next morning. I do a lot of repetitions to keep my upper body toned. Quickness is such a part of my game that I don't want to do anything that might make me bulky and slow.

That private investigator probably wondered what he was doing sitting around all that time I was working out. He must have found that part of his job to be pretty boring.

I want every team in the league to interview Dennis Rodman, to see what he's all about and what he's thinking. Chicago did that before they made the trade, and what happened? They made the trade. They put me through a three-day interview, sort of a tryout for the mind. They talked to former teammates of mine, former coaches, friends. They went all out. I don't always give people much when I meet with them, but when they take the time, they get a totally different view of me.

People know ***I LOVE THE GAME.*** I love it for all the same reasons I loved it when I came into the league nine years ago as a fresh-faced kid with an unusual past. I love it for the basketball, but basketball now has totally changed. It's more about making money than worrying about the people who are playing the game, and I've come to the conclusion that's the way I have to be too.

They had some conservative people running the team in San Antonio, **guys who don't know anything about basketball.** Popovich looked at me and said, "Well, he's not a family man. His image isn't right for this team." They couldn't pull their heads out of their asses long enough to realize I was exactly what they should have wanted. He should have been standing there looking at me and saying, "We need this guy, because he's going to come in and do the job."

I'm the basketball version of a gravedigger. Rebounding and playing defense is like putting the bodies in the hole. Nobody else on the floor is going to devote his whole career to that, so pay me for doing what the other guys don't want to do. If you want to pay me to go out there and play scared, I'll play scared. If you want me to go out there and kill myself for the troops, I'm going to do that. I'm the one who does that. I save everybody's ass on that damned court. **I saved David Robinson's ass,** I save everybody's ass. I will take the heat so those guys can go out under the lights and do a job well. *If people can't see that, they can KISS MY ASS.*

The life of the athlete is temporary. You get a lot in a short period of time—a lot of money, women, attention—and then it's gone. There's a risk of being tricked into believing it's going to last forever, but you have to remind yourself not to trust it. You can't trust any of it—the money, the women, or the attention. In the end none of it lasts.

When a player's career ends, the league doesn't give a shit about him, bro. When you're used up, everybody moves on. The league wants you to play the good soldier for the time that you're playing, but after that, the lights are out and they're not home. They tell you to **go pick up the plastics for recycling.**

This life is like a swimming pool. You dive into the water, but you can't see how deep it is. The first time you dive in, it's like there's no bottom. You can go down and down and the water goes on forever. Then you get tired, and you get out for a rest. The next time you dive in, everything looks the same but you crack your head on the bottom.

The problem is, you just never know when the depth of that pool is going to change.

There's no doubt this life is full of unique advantages. *If I was still working at the Dallas airport, I don't think I would have dated Madonna.* But there are disadvantages. There are dark sides to fame.

A player dreams of being a superstar, but he doesn't want people flocking all over him asking for an autograph. He doesn't want to run into a store to pick up something real quick and end up telling people they can't have his name scribbled on a piece of paper. Those people will remember that, too, and **in their minds YOU'LL BE AN ASSHOLE FOR LIFE.** There's nothing you can do to change their minds.

There are thousands of kids out there in the projects and the cities, thinking they're going to work hard and get a basketball scholarship. They're going to use the game to get out. I say great. I say go for it. A lot of people will tell you it's a lie, that you can't get out that way. They say nobody does. They have statistics and all that, but I say why not go for it? I got out that way, and as long as there is a living example of the dream, kids are going to chase it.

But if you're attempting to make it in the pros, you have to learn in college about what the NBA and professional life have to offer. You have to develop a sense of awareness of what you're getting into, because what you see from the outside isn't what you always get from the inside.

I can make a sixty-minute video that's going to show you a detailed look at what the NBA life—good and bad—is all about. It'll be a look you won't get from the league.

The video will tell them **_where the prostitutes are, where the drugs are, where the best women are._** I had to learn all this on the fly, by trial and error. I'd never been around anything even close to what I saw my rookie year with the Pistons. I went along with my eyes wide open, ready for anything, and I pretty much found whatever I wanted.

The NBA gives you a lot of different peepholes to look through. You put in your quarter and wonder, *What's the next show to come up?* It's always new and exciting, and you always keep throwing in more quarters. You think you're invincible with the fame and fortune, but you're still the same person.

The only difference is, **YOU'RE SELLING YOUR SOUL TO A BUSINESS, AND SOONER OR LATER, YOU'RE GOING TO GET BURNED.**

It takes only one thing to bring you down. It could be the money, it could be the whores, it could be your wife, your girlfriend—it could be anything. Something's going to suck you down; it's the price you pay for being in this business.

I've seen just about everything that's out there, and it's not easy to shock me. **Once you've had a total stranger ask you to fuck his wife while he watches, you're not going to be easily shocked.**

There's only one thing that shocks me: I'M STILL HERE. I was shocked that I got here, and I'm shocked that I'm still here. I don't know how long I expected to be in the league, but I do know that's all I expected: *to be in the league.* No rebounding titles, no Defensive Player of the Year awards. And I didn't expect the dramatic changes in the league today.

I've come to realize we are the prostitutes. We're professional prostitutes, wearing a game jersey and uniform, running seven miles in two hours. So if we've already established what we are, the only thing left to discuss is price. ***For five years I've felt like the best prostitute in a high-class whorehouse.*** I'm the one who brings the house all the johns and all the money, but every year it's the same:

All the other girls get paid more than I do.

five

The Lost Game

How a Great League Lost Its Way

There was one moment in my career that provides you with everything you need to know about me as a basketball player. It was late in the 1989–1990 season, the year we won our second straight league title in Detroit, and we were playing the Houston Rockets.

The game was tied with about a minute left. Hakeem Olajuwon beat me to the hoop and was going up for a dunk. I knew I was beat, but I couldn't let him have the easy basket. We never gave a team anything in those days. We defended every shot, fought for every rebound, and dove for every loose ball. As Hakeem went up, I came from behind and went up with him. He's taller than I am and stronger than I am, but I had the determination. I got right up there with him and blocked it. It was like I took it right out of the hoop.

When I realized what I had done, it was like everything stopped for a second. As soon as my hand hit the ball and slammed it away, I thought, **Did I really do what I think I did?** It was just so unbelievable for me to be able to do that, and the accomplishment overwhelmed me. I looked into the crowd and saw everybody staring with their mouths open, and I started to cry. *Right there on the court,* **I CRIED LIKE A BABY.** It was a moment of perfection, in line with my whole crazy life: I was beaten and given up for dead, but I made it back to shock the whole world.

And so I cried, right out there on the floor. I wasn't afraid to let my emotions show. I'm not so much of a tough guy that I would be embarrassed to cry in front of twenty-two thouand people. That's what I was feeling, so that's what I did: I cried. It was like it all came out of me at once. That one moment was a total capsule of everything I can do on the basketball court. I didn't give up, I fought like hell and I didn't let myself believe I couldn't make it.

I play with *real* emotion.

In the history of the NBA, you may never see any-body play with the kind of emotion I bring to the floor. You may never see anyone else who is willing to go out there and show all sides of himself, just be an open book in front of the whole world. Some guys talk about it, some guys think they show it, but how many really do it? How many can tell the difference between real emotion and the kind of emotion you practice in front of a mirror?

The common perception of me is that I'm this hard, tough guy—that I don't give a fuck about people or anything. But when you see me cry about something like not being able to see my daughter, you get a different idea. The emotion is raw, and there's nothing fake about it.

It's like the NBA thinks there's this great mystery out there: **Why do people like Dennis Rodman?** The people who don't know the answer to that question aren't in touch with the real people out there. They don't know what the people want to see. The working people, the people who have had to struggle to get something in their lives—they look at me and see someone who's one of them. **I go out there and get MY EYES GOUGED, MY NOSE BUSTED, MY BODY SLAMMED.** I love the pain of the game; it makes me feel alive. I've always loved pain, from the time we played football as kids on the asphalt of Oak Cliff. I'll go out there with blood running down my jersey or a bone sticking out of my arm, and I'll still be diving for loose balls. I'm tough, just like the mechanics and truck drivers and plumbers out there. They can relate. **I play balls-out,** and people appreciate that. They don't care about the other stuff, the stuff management wants them to care about.

I feel I have the power to express my sensitivity to everybody in the world, because everybody in the world feels the same way. They feel the pain, they feel the agony, they feel the stress. People can look at me and say, "There's someone who's not like all the other assholes in the NBA."

I'm not one of the pretty boys, and I'm not one of the biggest guys out there. I'm not even close to the biggest. I get beat up and banged up by guys like Charles Oakley and Kevin Willis, guys who have forty pounds or five inches on me—sometimes both. But the fan in the stands looks out there and sees that I'm the one with 20 rebounds at the end of the night, not the other guy. They look at me and say, "You know, he busts his ass like nobody else out there."

The league can market the pretty boys, but who do the people talk about when they're driving home from the arena? Dennis Rodman. I'm not trying to get attention by being flamboyant on the court; I'm playing the game the way it should be played. I'm doing it for the little kids who come to the game and say, "Mommy, Daddy, I like that guy with the green hair."

It's not just the hair or the tattoos, though. **If I colored my hair and went out there and played like Chris Dudley, nobody would give a shit about me.** You have to have stage presence and emotion, and you have to be able to make the people watching feel what you feel.

You have to bring the comedian out. You have to bring the seriousness out. You have to bring out all the sadness and all the happiness you have inside you. The game goes back and forth, with good stretches and bad stretches, and fans go through those same emotions when they're watching. If they watch me, I'll take them through every emotion the game has to offer. I might get mad and get a technical, I might get frustrated and knock Scottie Pippen into the bleachers, or I might get so happy that I stand out there and cry.

I had so many emotional moments when I played for the Pistons. I set the team's single-game rebounding record on March 4, 1992, when I had 34 rebounds against the Indiana Pacers. I had my radar going that game; I knew where every ball was headed, and I knew it before anybody else could react. The record I broke was set by Bob Lanier twenty years before. Bob Lanier was a six-foot-eleven, 270-pound center, one of the biggest men in the league. When I found out about this, **it made me so proud, I broke down and cried.**

After the game I was asked if this was the greatest achievement of my life. I said, "No, this isn't my greatest achievement. **THE GREATEST ACHIEVEMENT OF MY LIFE WAS TURNING MY LIFE AROUND."** It was true then, and it's true now.

Every time something big like that happens to me, I always think back to where I had been and how unlikely it was that I achieved anything more than a criminal record. Everything rushes back at me during those moments, and that's part of why I'm so emotional.

To me, the game can bring out that kind of emotion. **The game is sacred, almost holy.** I learned that in Detroit, where we played basketball the way it was supposed to be played. Every guy on that team wanted to play the right way. Everybody had a role, and it all came together to produce something beautiful on the court. We were the "Bad Boys" and we were physical and rough, but there's beauty in that to people who really understand the game.

Of all the things people have said about me over the years, the one thing they can't say is that I don't respect the game. They can criticize me for not conforming to their ideas of what's normal and right, but once I'm on the court, they can't take anything away from me.

I read one time where Dick Versace, Daly's assistant with the Pistons, said, "Nothing has ever affected Dennis's desire to win. He's never violated the sanctity of the game." That's pretty heavy stuff, and those are words I could never come up with, but it's the truest thing you could say about me. I've always cared about what happens on the court. The rest of it, to me, shouldn't matter.

The things I have accomplished on the court may never be repeated by someone my size. Before me no forward had ever won the NBA rebounding title twice in a row, and I'm at four times and counting. There were forwards who could rebound—Charles Barkley, Michael Cage, Truck Robinson—but nobody has ever come close to dominating the way I have. And I'm not leading the league by averaging twelve or thirteen rebounds a game; I'm over seventeen every year.

I think the NBA is getting away from pushing its players to achieve things like that. They're trying to create an image that takes all the emotion and all the teamwork out of the game. You may never see another guy who goes about his business like I do, rebounding and playing defense and letting the other guys score. There's a chance I wouldn't make it in the NBA if I was coming out right now, because it seems all anybody wants is a fancy scorer who they can market to their fans. The NBA right now is like a whole season of All-Star games. **Guys want to dunk and be flashy and see themselves on ESPN's SportsCenter every night.**

The teams themselves are contributing to this feeling. Walk into any arena in the league and look at what goes on outside the court. It seems the basketball is secondary. You get hit with a constant barrage of music and dance teams and stunts. **You've got guys flying off a trampoline to dunk a ball, you've got dancing gorillas and highlight shows during time-outs.** These things detract from the game. The entertainment might be okay during halftime and maybe even time-outs—I guess I can live with that—but you're seeing more teams pulling that shit during the game. *Public-address announcers are screaming* and **MUSIC IS BLASTING** while we're out there **TRYING TO PLAY THE FUCKING GAME.**

When I think back to when I first came into the league, back in 1986, the game was the most important thing. People came to see basketball. It's not the same now. They've taken the game and tried to turn it into a big family-entertainment center. Everything is geared toward making the family comfortable and happy. It takes away from the emotion of the game. If a home team calls a time-out after giving up a big run of points, the fans should be quiet and calm, maybe even pissed off. But the way it works now, nobody has time to be quiet. As soon as the whistle blows for the time out, **the dancers are running onto the court with big ol' smiles and the music is pumping like it's the Fourth of July.** Now everyone's supposed to be happy and smiling and dancing. What that tells me is the game doesn't really matter.

Winning has become secondary. Emotion has become secondary. We're putting on a show instead of being in a heated competition. The NBA believes if you can send the fans home happy, that's all that matters. The league thinks a few dunks is enough. It isn't, though. The game matters. You can entertain people and show them a good time by playing the game the way it should be played. **The game is enough. This is a great game.**

The league has gotten away from the things that made it great. The NBA's best years were from about 1981 to 1990, when guys like Magic Johnson, Larry Bird, and Isiah Thomas came into this league and brought it to the level of success and popularity is has today.

The league didn't get where it is by giving rookies $70 million contracts before they even play a minute in the league. It got there because of the game, and because there were people out there who knew how to play it. They loved the game and respected it. They cared about it. Is that too much to ask?

If it wasn't for guys like Bird, Magic, Michael, and Isiah—and guys like me too—the NBA would probably be behind baseball in terms of fan popularity. That would be a fucking disaster.

Or it could be even worse. If it wasn't for those guys and the teams they played on, the league could be dead right now. That time slot, from the beginning of the eighties to the beginning of the nineties, the league was provided with *basketball players.* These weren't showmen or guys who worried only about the way they looked on the highlights. Guys like Magic and Bird and Michael put on a great show, but it was always the team and the game that came first. Our Pistons team was a great example of a bunch of guys who went out there and knew the game, inside and out. You always knew where the other guy was going to be, and what he was going to do once he got there. **You watch some teams these days and you wonder if they just met on the playground and decided to choose up sides.**

When I go back and look at the tapes of those years—our games with the Celtics, the Lakers against the Celtics, us and the Bulls—it's all **flat-out, *BADASS BASKETBALL*.** It's guys playing hard, diving on the floor. It was Bird hitting jumpers in everybody's face, Isiah getting off shots inside, Laimbeer kicking somebody's ass, me shutting down Clyde Drexler or Bird or Scottie Pippen. It was the coolest time this sport ever knew.

The emotion of those playoff games against the Celtics or the Bulls was unlike anything I've ever been around. We were on a mission to beat those guys, and nothing else mattered. In San Antonio those guys couldn't block everything out and play like it was life or death. They didn't understand that you couldn't approach the playoffs like you approached the regular season. The heat was turned up in the playoffs, and you had to turn up the furnace inside you to compete.

Those Detroit teams were able to move everything off to the side in search of the championship. Kids had to move to the side, wives, girlfriends—anything that wasn't basketball. You just had to commit yourself and do without the distractions in order to make that dream come true. If you didn't, somebody would tell you about it. Rick Mahorn or Bill Laimbeer or somebody else would call you into a back room—I know they did it with me—and say, **"Yo, bro, get with the program. We're all in this together and you can't be fucking with it."**

Everyone had a feeling these were special years in the

NBA. It was an incredible collection of great players coming together at the same time to rescue the game. Before those years, the NBA was a wasteland. It was in danger of going out of business. **The league was a traveling cocaine show,** and teams weren't selling out every arena like they are today. Not even close.

It was incredible to be a part of the era when the league came alive, and to have been on one of the teams that made that era great. Today, guys don't know the game. All they know today is **how much MONEY, how much FAME, how much PUSSY** they can get. It's as simple as that. Who has the best cars? Who has the best clothes? Who can get there first with the most?

The game? **FUCK THE GAME.**

You can go around the league and pick out the people like that. The rookies coming in don't know the game. They're coming into the league too early, and they're getting all this money and there's no incentive to learn the game. There are examples everywhere. Guys like **Rasheed Wallace and Glenn Robinson are** good players, but they're **not ready to come in and take over the league** like everyone is led to believe.

I understand that players have a lot of money, and everybody wants to dress nicely and have a cool car, but goddamn, care about the game. Please care about the game.

It makes me sad to see the game today. It's like we worked so hard to bring it up to a certain level, and then it got out of hand. Things got out of control and it started sliding backward. **THE LEAGUE TODAY IS VERY, VERY UNHEALTHY.** Most of the guys who come into the league buy into the image of what the league is selling, and they're going to regret it. That life provides you with nothing but a lifelong hole inside you. There's going to be a hole in your life you can't heal up. It's going to grow and grow and grow until it's so fucking big, no doctor's going to be able to stitch it up.

The hole is created when you've got the opportunity

and the wide range to have everything in your life. Everything. There are no rules and no boundaries to the things you can experience. But when that stretch of time is over, when you're all used up and nobody wants your autograph anymore, what have you done to prepare your mind to fill this fucking hole? There's nothing out there to prepare you to fill it.

More than anything this game is a diversion. It's an escape. The people who watch us love the game because it takes them out of their daily routine. They can put aside the problems with their husbands, wives, kids, and bosses for two hours of entertainment.

The NBA has discovered it can make money this way. You can sell jerseys and posters based on highlight clips and images on the television screen. The league has removed the pressure to perform. **The feeling in that Pistons locker room—that charged energy—wasn't in the Spurs locker room.** I think it was in Houston, because Hakeem put it there, and it's in Chicago with the Bulls, but in most places I don't think it exists.

The downfall started when they decided it was a good idea to give rookies insane amounts of money before they got into the league. It should be just like baseball used to be: If you performed, you got paid. They've taken that carrot away, and they've started gearing the game more for the attraction and the profit than the basketball.

Money changes everybody. Anybody who says different is lying. It changed me at the beginning of my career, when I got to Detroit and got my first paycheck. I had never had money before. I used to think the $6.50 an hour I made at the airport was a fortune. Now I was looking at a salary of about $110,000, and all of a sudden the world was different. I could do—and buy—shit I never knew existed before.

But it never changed me as a player. And if it did, there were guys on that team that would have steered me in the right direction in no time. The reasons I was playing the

**Is Glenn Robinson worth $9 million a year?
I DON'T *THINK* SO**

game have always stayed the same. The game was all I cared about; it never felt like a job. **After the shit I'd been through, how could I ever think of basketball as a job?**

Glenn Robinson came into the league and started making $9 million right off the bat. Chris Webber signed a $68 million contract with the Golden State Warriors when he left Michigan and was the first pick in the 1993 draft. Look at the first five or six picks of every draft for the past five or six years and you'll see incredible amounts of money being given to players who hadn't achieved anything.

The game has been hurt by this. ***The players coming into the league in the nineties aren't as well rounded*** as they were ten years ago. Aside from guys like Jason Kidd or Anfernee Hardaway, everybody who comes in thinks all you have to do is score and look good and everybody will love you. The young players aren't working as hard to get better, either, because all that money is guaranteed. They could score one point a game for the rest of their lives and still cash the checks.

92

Why do you need to compete and work your ass off if you're making $80 million over ten years, and every cent of it is guaranteed?

I *think* the league is headed for trouble. It's fine now—the teams are making money, the sport is still popular—but they're trying to bring a new image to the game and I think it's going to blow up in their faces at some point.

It's similar to what happened to us in Detroit. We were the "Bad Boys"—me, Laimbeer, Mahorn, Salley—and the league thought that was cool. They marketed us as the "Bad Boys" and people started picking up on it. Everywhere we went it was "Bad Boys" this and "Bad Boys" that. We loved it and thrived off it. Then, after about

**Chris Webber? $68 million?
I DON'T *THINK* SO**

two years of this, the NBA changed its mind. It wasn't a good idea to promote "Bad Boys" anymore, so they dropped it. We were the same guys, playing the same way, but I guess we weren't "Bad Boys" anymore because we'd lost the blessing of the league office. We were setting a bad example for kids, probably, because we were playing the game the way it should have been played. Incredible.

THE NBA IS AFRAID OF ME.

The people at the top of the league think they need to rein me in so I don't become another Michael Jordan, somebody they aren't able to mold and shape and make their puppet.

The NBA didn't make me. They're in the business of taking these young guys who come into the league and marketing the hell out of them until they become stars. They take the guys everybody knows from college, and they throw them into the spotlight right away. They choose the players they think show the NBA in the most positive light so everybody buys jerseys with their names on them and votes them into the All-Star Game.

They create the image, then they control the image.

But they didn't create me, and they can't control me.

I didn't need the league's help to get where I am. I made it in spite of them, bro. It seems the league and the Spurs were trying to discourage people from liking me, and what happened? It backfired. *Sports Illustrated* ran a cover story of me in May of 1995—the one with me wearing leather on my body and one of my fifteen exotic birds on my shoulder—that was the best-selling *Sports Illustrated* of the year, if you don't count the swimsuit edition. That's the kind of thing the league doesn't understand. *SOMETIMES DIFFERENT IS BETTER.*

I honestly don't think the league wants guys to take the

route I did,
to come from nothing
and build it up on my own. The
guys who run the league are scared by
that, because they want to control the image and control
the person.

For seven years in this league I was seen as a guy who won a couple of rebounding titles, always played harder than shit, and spoke his mind. That was basically it. I wasn't a threat to anybody, and it didn't look like I would make a huge dent in the league. I did things like hang out in Vegas, losing money faster than thought, and get my daughter's portrait tattooed into my forearm. I was a novelty, but nobody thought it would amount to much more than that.

Then, all of a sudden, that changed. After that night in the parking lot of The Palace, I made the decision to be the person I wanted to be, and not the person everybody else wanted me to be. Or the person everyone thought I was going to become.

When I first got to San Antonio, I changed my hair. I wasn't trying to make a statement, really, it was just something to do. I went to a hairdresser in San Antonio, and he and I talked about it. I had dreadlocks at the time, and I told him I wanted to make a bold statement. I decided to bleach my hair blond.

I had it done on the day they unveiled the Alamodome; all the team investors, tons of media, and about five thousand fans were there to watch us go through drills and shoot around. I was thirty minutes late because the damned bleach job took too long. When I finally got to the arena, they introduced me and I took off my RODMAN EXCAVATION cap and let the world see the new me. The place went absolutely nuts.

David Robinson introduced me and handed me the microphone.

"You can like me or hate me," I said. "But all I can say is, **when I get on that damn floor, all I'm going to do is get *solid.*"**

That's all I said. I just dropped the microphone on the floor and walked off.

When I saw how the people responded to me, I realized, this is the time to break out, the time to be who I really want to be. People accepted this. They started calling me "Demolition Man" in San Antonio, after the Wesley Snipes movie.

The funny thing is, everybody thought I was copying Wesley Snipes when I first did my hair that way, but I didn't know anything about that movie until afterward. I went to it, and when I saw him I thought, *Oh, shit*, that's *what everybody's talking about.*

What I did when I got to San Antonio was totally change my persona, and the persona of the game changed with me. It was nothing to go from there to red hair, or orange hair, or green hair with the red AIDS ribbon colored into the back of my head. People came to expect something from me. **THEY HAD CALL-IN POLLS ABOUT MY HAIR COLOR**— all that shit. It was like a damned brushfire that nobody could control.

This scared the NBA. This was out of their control. I was coloring outside the lines, and the league didn't know where it would lead next.

I know what scared them: they were afraid I might bring something totally different back to this game, and that's dignity. Dignity for all the players. Being human. They're afraid of that. They don't want to see guys going out there and getting tattoos or voicing their opinions. When I first got a tattoo, there were very few guys in the league—or in all of sports—with tattoos. Now look around. Everybody's got one. I'm not unique anymore, even though **I'm still leading the league with eleven.** Just about every other guy in college has a tattoo now. Players like Damon Stoudamire come into the league with tattoos and nobody even notices them. Dennis Scott got his father's image tattooed onto his arm and it wasn't a big deal. Some players are bringing something different to the floor, and you'd have to be blind to think I didn't have at least a little something to do with that.

The bottom line is, this league wants to control its players. They want to restrict players from doing things that are natural and human to do. They don't want anybody insulting the people who buy the tickets—the wealthy corporate types, because they're the only ones who can afford to go anymore. Nobody wants somebody like me around, stepping on toes, making mistakes and doing normal, human things.

They want ROBOTS who can DUNK.

The NBA is so big on marketing. They were ahead of football and baseball from the start. The league understood what could happen if it flooded people with positive images of the top players. But they've gotten so limited in who they market that it's almost suffocating. Mostly it's **Michael and Shaq.** They force those two guys down people's throats. Pretty soon it's like, okay, nothing but *Michael and Shaq, Michael and Shaq.* Maybe some Grant Hill mixed in. How much of that can you take? The NBA's also hypocritical. They tell players all the things they can't do—you can't swear on the court, you can't be rough with the league's chosen ones—but, at the same time, **they're lining their pockets every time I do something out of the ordinary.** Every time they make a big deal out of something, they profit from it. That happened in the 1991 playoffs, when I bumped Scottie Pippen into the stands, which cut his chin and cost me $5,000. It happened again in the 1994 playoffs, when I threw a hip at John Stockton and they suspended me for a game. More people get interested in the games when they can advertise me as the NBA's bad boy. More people come out to see me play. More people turn on the television to watch, and they can use the ratings to get more money from the people who advertise. I know how the system works.

It's almost like the league is saying, "Okay, we'll let you go to a certain point, as long as it's good for us, *then we're going to have to sit on you and make you look like an asshole.*" When they do that, they look good both ways. They make their money, and they also give the public the impression they can control me.

To me, they're saying I can't be a man. That's what it comes down to: You just cannot be a man. You have to be what they think a man is. You have to be what an "NBA Man" is supposed to be.

The guys making these rules are guys like **David Stern**—fifty-year-old white men who didn't come from where I came from, and didn't come from where most of the NBA players came from. They don't understand anything but the business part of the sport. They don't understand the emotion and the intensity that goes into being a player in this league. Look, if a guy wants to get pissed off, let him get pissed off. I want to ask the league: **WHAT ARE YOU AFRAID OF**—That somebody might show they care about this game?

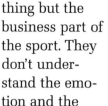

David Stern: fifty-year-old white guys make all the rules.

There are too many guys in the league like fucking Karl Malone, guys who are too high class to say anything to me.

They're too fucking white collar to bother with some lowlife bum like me. They can't "associate" with me off the court because I'm too different. I don't wear the custom clothes and go to the

Karl Malone's too high-class for a bum like me.

99

right parties. I hang out with real people in real places, and they can't let anyone like that into their fucking club.

And the part that pisses them off the most is this: **I DON'T GIVE A SHIT.** Don't talk to me, because I don't want to talk to your ass anyway. Don't invite me to your fucking parties, because I won't come.

A lot of players in the league are afraid of me—especially the guys just coming in. They've read about, or heard about, me roughing people up on the court or sleeping in my truck with a loaded rifle or dating Madonna. They get out onto the floor and look into my eyes, and they don't know what to expect. That's my edge against them. I keep the edge sharp by not talking to anybody on the court. I don't talk to anybody on the other team, and I rarely talk to the guys on my own team. These guys look at me and they're amazed at what I do, and they're a little intimidated by the way I do it.

I've had quite a few players come up to me and say, **"WHAT DRIVES YOU, BRO?** What keeps you going like that? How can you run all fucking night, diving all over the floor, and never get tired?" All the time they're asking these questions, they're looking at me like they're not sure they really want to know.

Then there are the guys like Charles Barkley. I can't count the number of times he's come up to me and said, "I wish I had you two years ago. You have it all, bro. You just have it *all.*" We came so close to playing together too. Before the Pistons traded me to San Antonio, they had made a deal to send me to Phoenix for Richard Dumas. Then Dumas tested positive for drugs and the trade was called off. Just another bad break. **CAN YOU IMAGINE CHARLES BARKLEY AND ME IN THE SAME STARTING LINE-UP?** Would *anybody* get a rebound against us?

It seems the one time other players want to talk to me is when they decide it's time to preach to me. These are **the churchgoing, conservative guys:**

David Robinson, Hakeem Olajuwon, Avery Johnson. Karl Malone even lowered himself to do it one time, but it was a long time ago. They try to talk to me, and each time I just look at them and either nod or shake my head. I don't have anything to say to them, and they **come away thinking I'm CRAZY.**

I know what they want, and I'm not going to give them the satisfaction of getting it. They want to hear me roar. They want to hear me say things nobody else will say. They want me to confirm in their minds that **I'M AS WEIRD AS THEY THINK I AM.**

"Dennis, we gotta talk," they'll say. "You've got to set an example for the kids."

They might as well just come out and say, "What's driving you? What's making you *mad*?" That's the word they use to describe me: *mad*.

The ridiculous thing about these "NBA stars" worrying about the example I set for kids is the response I get from kids. It's the complete opposite of everything I hear from the league and its so-called important players.

Kids tell me, "I think you're so cool."

I don't hear, "I think you're a great basketball player." There's a big difference between "I love your style," and "I love the way you rebound." To me it means they're getting something from me that isn't completely or only about basketball.

I wonder, why are there people out there who idolize Dennis Rodman? Why? It baffles me. There's a lady in Los Angeles, a high-class hairstylist at a big-time salon in Beverly Hills, who joined my fan club in San Antonio and called me at the hotel one time when I was in Los Angeles. I met with her—no sex, nothing like that—and we had dinner. Now I see her when I come to Los Angeles. She told me to come in and have my nails done at her salon, so one Saturday afternoon when I was living in Orange County I decided to drive into Beverly Hills and do it. I didn't know the first thing about where she worked, and it turned out to be this ritzy, famous place called Umberto, a block off Rodeo Drive. **I'm feeling way out of place getting my nails painted in this place—cobalt-blue, by the way.**

But it's people like her that make me wonder, what's the attraction? *Sometimes I don't even know who I am, and these people are calling me their hero?* But when I ask them why, almost all of them say the same thing: "You're your own man. You just don't give a fuck what anybody thinks."

Charles Barkley got crucified for saying he isn't a role model, but I'm not either. I'm not trying to be a role model. I know I'm in a position where I should be one, but I'm not. I can't put myself up there on that pedestal and tell kids they should do things the way I do them. I know my way isn't for everybody, and **I would hope that everybody has an easier road to success than I had.** I figure the only thing I can do is show that I care about people and that you can be in the public spotlight and still be true to yourself.

THIS ROLE-MODEL BUSINESS IS MOSTLY HYPOCRITICAL BULLSHIT, anyway. You make it to the NBA, so you've got to be this big-ass poster child now. If you sit at the end of the bench, you don't have to be as much of a role model, but if you're good, you've got to really put some effort into it.

When you make it, you've got to go out there and **do public service** and **make donations** and **start foundations.** A lot of that stuff doesn't mean shit, though. Guys aren't setting up these nonprofit foundations or making appearances at soup kitchens because they want to. They're doing it because somebody's telling them it's *good for their image* and they might be able to make some money off it someday.

I don't have a foundation, and I don't give ten bucks for every rebound, but **I do things nobody else does.** I give tickets to people on the street who might never see an NBA game because they've priced the damned seats out of everybody's range. I've given tickets to homeless families who are standing outside arenas begging for food. I've done this all over: San Antonio, Boston, New York. I used to do it all the time in Detroit. I just walk up to these people and ask them if they'd like to see a game. Most of the time they're so stunned that somebody like me would talk to them that they can't do much more than nod.

I like to go into the toughest parts of town, wherever I am, just to remember where I came from. I do it all the time in Dallas, just go back and walk or drive through my old neighborhood. In Detroit I used to give out money all the time—just hand it out because those people need it more than I do. I talk to people, too, because I can relate to them. I know what it's like to be out there with nothing. One time **I gave this man on a street corner in Detroit close to a thousand dollars.** It was all I had in my pocket, and what the fuck did I need it for? This guy had a hard life, and he had nothing to show for it. I do those things to keep myself balanced, and to stay in touch with the real world. Sometimes I'd strike up a conversation with somebody on the streets and bring him home with me. I'd just tell him to get in the car and come home with me. Then I would feed him and let him clean himself up. It doesn't take much to make a difference in somebody's life. In this world of professional basketball, you can wall yourself off and make believe there's no suffering in the world.

To me, what I do is affecting people more directly than if I put my name on some charity just so I can look good. I watch other players, guys who do all the right public-service things, and they'll cross the street to avoid making eye contact with the kind of people I give tickets or food to.

Just show by example. It's that easy. You don't have to do all that other crap, especially if you're not comfortable with it. I don't think it's fair for people to put us on this pedestal and say, "You've got to be a good boy for the ten years you play in this league. You behave for ten years and be a role model."

I'm sitting here looking at how all this works and I'm thinking, Damn . . . *really?*

I have some questions about this format. Does it mean that all of a sudden I've got to run your life because I'm an athlete? I have to make you believe everything's great because I'm an athlete now? Maybe it's not great. **Maybe my life isn't great.** If I tell you it is, I'm lying to you. **Is lying okay because I'm carrying out my duties as a role model?**

Is it fair for me to pretend I can give you the leadership, the guidance, and the direction just because I can play this game? How did you function before I got here? How did you make it to work or school or wherever you go before I came along? Did you have a great life or a bad life and now—just because you found somebody you really love, idolize, and emulate—you want to trademark yourself as that person? Do you really want to wear that person's jersey and pretend you're him just because he can play a game?

I don't think that's the way it's supposed to work. **WE'RE ATHLETES.** We're not equipped to run somebody else's life. That's not our occupation. **We don't have all the answers, BRO.** Maybe some of us are the ones still asking questions. If you look at it from my side, **why should I try to make you believe in the things I believe in?** If I do that, I'm setting myself up for a big fall. There are people out there with a bomb, waiting for a guy like me to fail. When you do fail, they say, "Oh, I knew that was going to happen. I knew it. Why did I ever trust this person? Why did I ever believe he wouldn't fail me?"

Society is so messed up today. **Kids have too much to get into right in their own**

neighborhoods to worry about what I'm doing. The NBA's chosen ones think I'm setting a bad example? I think they need to look around and stop taking themselves so seriously. You're just not that important, bro.

Drugs are running wild, like a fucking river down the street. Girls are getting pregnant younger and younger, and AIDS doesn't give a shit how old you are. As my daughter, Alexis, grows up, I know she's going to get in trouble. I can teach her everything I know. I can tell her the way it is: **IF YOU'RE GOING TO HAVE SEX, USE A CONDOM.** Be safe. Be careful. I can't tell her not to have sex. If I do, she's going to do it anyway. She's going to do it just to spite me. All I can do is coach her and tell her the options.

I think kids respect you more when you put the decision in their hands. If you tell them they can have sex, but they have to be careful, they're going to look at that and say, "He says I can have sex, but you know what? If I don't want to, I don't have to."

WITH ME, EVERYTHING'S RIGHT ON THE TABLE. You can accept it or ignore it a lot easier when you know there's no hypocrisy involved. I just try to entertain the people and stay true to myself and the game. I don't preach to kids, I don't talk to kids. I do know that every kid is looking for an escape. They're looking for something that's outside their world, whether they're living in the worst project or the ritziest suburb. **I spent my whole childhood looking for an escape,** and I didn't find it until I started growing and playing basketball after high school. Even then it was like *the escape found me.*

I was confused as a kid. **I was *confused* ABOUT MY SEXUAL IDENTITY,** my future—my whole place in the world. But I didn't know what I wanted. When you grow up in the projects, the world seems so small. Your mind is not trained to look down the line. You don't reason out what might happen if you turn right, or what might happen if you turn left. There's nothing in your frame of reference for things like consequences or goals. Most kids are like that, to some degree or another. You're just a kid, living day to day, and you have to make all those mistakes and find your path on your own. ***No athlete can help you do that,*** and I think **IT'S STUPID AND EGOTISTICAL FOR US TO THINK WE CAN.**

six

Dirty Work

The World's Greatest Rebounder

I **NEVER WANT TO SCORE.** Never. I want to rebound. I want to break the record for most consecutive years leading the league in rebounding. If I do that, they'll have to say I was one of the best who ever played. Then when it comes time to get me into the Hall of Fame, they'll throw a Pete Rose at me and find an excuse to keep me out.

Moses Malone holds the record for most consecutive years leading the league in rebounding, with five. I came to the Bulls with four to my name, and I honestly think I'm just starting to perfect my craft. If I break Malone's record, I think it would be *the most incredible record in basketball history*—more incredible than Michael Jordan winning the scoring title seven years in a row; more incredible than Wilt

Chamberlain averaging twenty rebounds a game for eight years in a row.

Bigger than all that, bro, and here's why:

I've taken one part of the game and made it into an art form. I've taken this ugly stepchild and made it beautiful. Rebounding is grunt work—like working the graveyard shift as an airport janitor—and now it's being recognized as a pivotal, elegant part of the game.

Who wants to rebound? NOBODY. Who wants to score? EVERYBODY.

I saw that when I came into the league, plain as day. Rebounding drills were no fun. It was no fun to have everybody climbing over your back while you try to move somebody out of the way with your ass and keep your hands in position

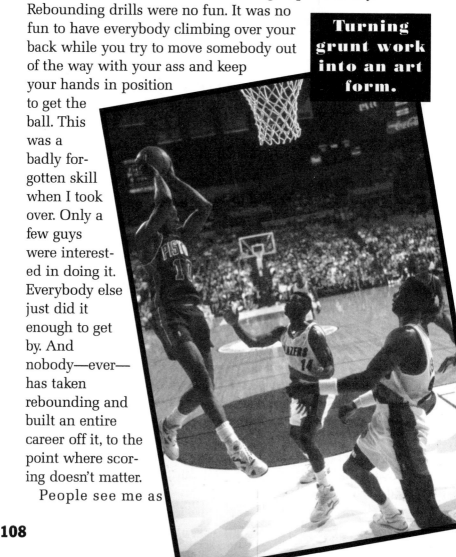

Turning grunt work into an art form.

to get the ball. This was a badly for- gotten skill when I took over. Only a few guys were interest- ed in doing it. Everybody else just did it enough to get by. And nobody—ever— has taken rebounding and built an entire career off it, to the point where scor- ing doesn't matter.

People see me as

high strung, flamboyant, wild, crazy—you name it—but they love to see me out there perfecting my craft.

Through me the world has recognized how important rebounding is to the game of basketball. My career is filled with examples of my team playing much better, and winning much more, when I'm in the lineup:

- I moved into the starting lineup in my second year in Detroit, after Adrian Dantley injured an ankle **We won 20 of the first 24 games** I started.

- In my last year with the Pistons, probably the most screwed-up year I've had, I missed twenty games. We lost 16 of those 20 games. At one point that year **we were 17–12 when I played and 0–12 when I didn't.**

- In 1994–95 with the Spurs, my last year there, **I played in 49 games. We won 43 of them** and ended up with the best record in the NBA. After the Spurs traded me to Chicago, they couldn't keep up that pace. At the same time the Bulls picked up their pace.

I've heard about high school and college coaches who want to thank me for making rebounding cool again. Those coaches might think I'm a coach's worst nightmare, but they appreciate what I've done for this part of the game. **KIDS WANT TO REBOUND AGAIN,** because I've brought it out of the shadows.

Other players come up to me and want to talk rebounding. It's like they're saying, "I need to talk to this genius to see what he has to say. What's driving him? What's making him *mad*?" That's the word I hear the most—*mad*.

I don't give those guys much. I don't talk to the opponent. I just tell them, **"IT'S GOT TO BE INSIDE YOU, bro.** If it isn't inside you, it's not going to come out of you."

Somebody asked Isiah Thomas about me when I was going through hell my last year in Detroit, and Isiah said,

"I really think that Dennis is a kind of genius."

How many players in the history of the league have totally revolutionized a particular part of the game? Wilt Chamberlain was a great rebounder, but he was standing a head taller than everybody else, at a time when the league's shooting percentages were down in the mid-30-percent range. Today the league shooting percentage is up around 50 percent, so there are a lot fewer balls coming off the rim to begin with.

Bill Russell made the blocked shot an art form. He was the first guy who figured out how to block the shot and keep it in play for his teammates. What he did, in a way, was combine a blocked shot and a rebound. His blocks ended up as outlet passes because he was so damned good at directing the ball to teammates.

But really, who else? Michael Jordan has done tremendous things for the game, but Julius Erving was dunking like that ten years before Michael showed up. And dunking, as entertaining as it is, isn't any more important than any other shot. **It's art, but it's still only** two **points.**

For the past five years, any discussion of rebounding has to start with me. And I'm the opposite of Wilt Chamberlain; those guys he looked down on are the guys I'm looking up to now. At six foot eight and 220 pounds I'm one of the smallest power forwards in the league.

The first thing I hear from people I see out in public is this: **You're too small.** That's what they say, that I'm too small for my accomplishments. People expect me to look like Charles Oakley or something—big and wide. I'm skinny at 220 pounds, and I'm way too small to be in there pounding it out with the guys like Oakley, who's six foot nine and 250 pounds.

Also, I accentuate the rebounding by not scoring. The teams I play for don't need me to score. There's always somebody out there who can score—Isiah Thomas could score, David Robinson could score, Jordan and Scottie Pippen could score—but **THERE'S NOBODY OUT**

THERE WHO CAN DO WHAT I DO.

Someday I'd love to be the first player in the game's history to average eighteen rebounds a game and only two points.

To me it would be perfect. It's like turning the game on its head. People would say, **"How'd he do that?"** How the hell can he turn a game around without even scoring a point—without even trying to?" I think that would blow people away.

Whenever anyone would ask about my scoring ability, Chuck Daly used to say, "Dennis doesn't even need to score to make a major difference in the game." He used to say having me on the team made the difference in anywhere from six to ten games a season.

And if you look closer, you'll see I do more than rebound. I coach. I choreograph everything on the floor. It's not by word, it's by knowing the game and knowing where everybody should be. I don't talk to my teammates much off the court, but I'm talking all the time on the court. **I'M VERY SERIOUS ABOUT MY BASKETBALL.** I still go back to the things James Rich taught me in Oklahoma: **Go all out for what you want, and damn anybody who gets in your way.**

The other team has to watch me every second. I'm giving my team a second chance every time. It's like saying you've got an atomic bomb right here that can go off at any time, any moment. Before I came along, nobody realized how powerful a rebounder could be in shaping the game.

The elements that make a great rebounder are pretty simple. Rebounding is desire, hustle, hard work, talent, intelligence—all of those things. There's also something instinctive about it. I think you have to have a sense of where the ball is going to come down. I really do think it's something that's inside you.

In 1991–92, I averaged 18.7 rebounds a game and had 20 or more rebounds in a game 39 times. Think about that: almost half the season with at least 20 rebounds a game. That was the year I broke the Pistons' single-game record by pulling down 34 in a game against the Indiana Pacers. In that game—hell, in that whole season—I felt like I knew exactly how every shot was going to come off the rim.

I think I've always been able to predict things. I think it has a lot to do with aggressiveness and alertness, but it also gets back to desire. I'm hungrier than those other guys out there. Every rebound is a personal challenge. I train my mind to believe **I need to get every rebound just to stay in the league. If I don't get the ball, I'm going back to Dallas, back to the streets, back to that hell.** I think of myself as a lion or any other wild animal in the jungle. They go after their prey for survival. If an animal's hungry enough, it's going to attack anything that moves.

I see a ball out there, I'm going to get it. Simple, but how many guys go all-out to do it?

My desire is always there, but as my career goes along I have to work at it a little more. The way the league has changed, and the way teams have treated me have taken some of the thrill from the game. It's harder at thirty-four years old than it was at twenty-six. I force myself to believe I'm still hungry, that what happens on that court still matters. I can't stop and tell you why I want it, but I still do. ***I'm fighting against becoming soft.*** To me, that's the worst thing you can say to a basketball player, even worse than running down his mother.

Sometimes I'm not even satisfied when I got 6 points and 22 rebounds, because I'm always looking to do more. I hate to see another guy get a rebound. I look at him as somebody who's trying to send me out of this league, back to where I came from.

In a weird way, **I became a great rebounder and one-on-one defender by sitting on the bench** as a rookie with the Pistons. I had all this energy, and I was just sitting there, watching everybody else play. I couldn't let the energy out, except in practice, and that wasn't good enough.

I played in 77 of the 82 games my rookie year, but I averaged only fifteen minutes a game. There was no way I was going to sit that much again—I wouldn't have survived.

I looked at my team and I looked around the league, and **I MADE A DECISION:** I could be the best in the world at rebounding if I was willing to work hard enough at it. I saw then that rebounding was something guys did only so they could run back down and score. I knew it was my ticket to a career.

When I was in college, rebounding was something I did without thinking. I averaged almost 16 rebounds at game at Southeastern, and I was scoring more than 25 a game too. I was such a better athlete than everybody at that level that I could get 15 rebounds a game just by showing up.

At first, the decision to focus on rebounding was about survival. At the start of my second year in the league, I told myself, "I have to do the things nobody wants to do. I've got to do that to stay in this league." Those two things were rebounding and defense. At the time the decision was pretty basic: I didn't think I could stay in the league without adding something to my game.

So every day I'd go to practice and play my teammates, who were also some of the best guys in the league—Adrian Dantley, John Salley, Rick Mahorn. When I first got there, **they used to *beat* my ASS,** but eventually I stopped them a couple of times. It kind of shocked me, but it made me come out the next day and say, "Goddamn, I can do this. It's a lot of hard work, but *I CAN DO THIS.*" And every day I got more confident and more confident, and it started to happen.

Every time we scrimmaged, I would go up against the first-teamers and look at every possession like it was survival. If I stopped Dantley this time down the floor, I'd get to stay in the league. If I got the next rebound, I'd stay in the league. I started thinking like that, and the guys I was playing against started looking at me like I was crazy. These were veterans, and they knew how to practice without killing themselves. Now they were faced with **this WILD-ASS KID who was playing every second like it was his last.**

Chuck Daly encouraged me to do this. It was fine with him that I wasn't interested in scoring, and he put a lot of energy into telling me how good I could be if I didn't let myself get off track. Whenever I was down, he'd always find the right way to tell me to pick my head up. The man kept me going.

I started to visualize all these great players I would guard, and how I would guard them. I'd watch films, and I made myself believe that I stopped these guys before I even played them. I'd put myself on the floor in the videotape, and I'd go over play it in my mind, and **I'D STOP THEM EVERY TIME.** My mind started to respond to that, and those things I visualized started happening on the court.

My rookie year **I was very immature.** I didn't know the game of basketball, and I didn't know how to focus myself in the right direction. I saw everybody scoring, and there were times when I thought that's what I would have to do to stay in the league. I took a chance by basing everything in my career on rebounding and defense, because not everybody sees how important those things are. If they have a guy who can score twelve points a game, grab eight rebounds, and play decent defense, some coaches would rather keep him than a guy like me. The safe choice is to go with the basic, everyday guy and not the guy who does something unusual.

My second year I played more and averaged 8.7 rebounds a game. That was my big scoring year too—11.6 a game. That could be the answer to a trivia question someday: **HOW MANY YEARS DID DENNIS RODMAN AVERAGE MORE POINTS THAN REBOUNDS IN A SEASON?** That's it, one—1987–88.

Chuck Daly used to tell me, "**Opportunity comes to**

people who wait." When I was a rookie, sitting on the bench with all that energy, I thought that was **BULLSHIT.** I thought opportunity came to people who went out and took it.

Now I believe what Daly said. I was just so antsy to play that I couldn't think straight about anything. All this energy needed to be let out, and it wasn't getting the chance. It wasn't that I wanted to play just so I could show my stuff. I wanted to play so I could get rid of the energy.

In my younger years, when I was twenty-six up to about thirty years old, I had more energy to jump. *I was a* *FUCKING RABBIT.* Now I'm not worried about jumping like that. Sometimes I can't believe more players don't do what I do on the court, because it seems so damn basic to me. You don't have to jump out of the gym to get a rebound; you just have to keep at it.

I don't worry that much about positioning, because I'm at a size disadvantage to begin with. I'll look for my man to block out, but most of the time I've read where the ball's going to go before he has, so it makes more sense for me to get after the ball instead of my man. I led the league in offensive rebounds four years in a row, mostly because that's when you have free rein to go for the ball and not worry about your man.

The one thing I do that nobody else *does* is jump three and four times for one rebound. I stay with the ball and control it by tipping it closer and closer to myself, until I get it close enough to get both hands on. I've got a quick jump—one of the quickest. I can get down on the floor and back up in the air faster than **a** **pogo stick.** Most people think you have to jump high to get a rebound, but jumping quickly is more important. I can jump and tip, jump and tip, jump and tip— boom! boom! boom!—three times in the time it takes the other guy to jump once. That's the key. It takes some concentration and body control to keep your head up and stay with the ball the whole time. It also takes conditioning, because a lot of guys get slow and tired after the second jump. They're the ones taking a deep breath when I'm launching into my third or fourth jump.

I've probably lost about 15 percent of my jumping ability over the years, if I had to put a number on it. But I've gained the confidence and the intelligence to change up and continue to be great. I don't have to jump over somebody, because now I can go around them or through them. A lot of times I'll be in poor rebounding position, boxed out by a bigger player, but I'll end up with the ball because I wait until my opponent jumps, and if he doesn't read the ball just perfectly I go up over him and tip the ball to myself. It's all a part of adapting to what you have and what the other guy gives you on the court. Some guys get great position, but they can't time their jumps to save their life. I let those guys have their position, then **I EAT THEM ALIVE FROM BEHIND.**

It's the same as a baseball pitcher losing his fastball; he can still throw hard, but he has to mix it up a little more to get people out.

In 1991–92, the year I won my first rebounding title, Kevin Willis of the Hawks started out like a wild man. Twenty games into the season he was averaging 18.5 rebounds a game and I was averaging around 11.

To me, **11 rebounds is like not even playing.** I looked at the statistics sheet before a game and realized how bullshit it was that I was that far behind. I can remember going into the rest room—I don't remember where, but I remember the rest room—and having a conversation with myself.

"You know, something is really off here," I told myself. "What am I doing wrong?"

I had started to doubt myself. Later, I was telling a friend about this and he said, "You're going to catch that guy. Before the All-Star break, you'll be leading the league in rebounds. Mark my word."

"You sure about that, bro?"

He said, "Yeah. I'm sure."

I went back to the drawing board with myself. I started

looking at videotapes ,videotapes, videotapes. I do that anyway, all the time, but this time I was searching for something. **I was searching for myself,** in a way. I knew I needed to find other ways, other options, for getting to the ball.

Then, all of a sudden, I had one big game of 29 rebounds. I couldn't pinpoint what the difference was, but during that game, I was telling myself, "Yeah, this is it. I found it." It was like I broke through, and there was no stopping me. I was getting between guys and over guys and through guys to get the rebounds. There were nine other guys out there, but I felt like **I WAS ALL ALONE ON THAT COURT.**

The next game I had another 20 rebounds, the next game 20 rebounds, the next game 20 rebounds. Six games straight I had 20 rebounds, and the next thing you know I'm leading the league in rebounds—before the All-Star break.

I made the All-Star Game that year and averaged 18.7 rebounds a game. There was some talk, about sixty games into the season, that I could be the first guy in a long time to average 20 rebounds a game. I was over 19 a game going into the last month, but I faded a little toward the end.

From there I started building my craft. Some games I would have four rebounds at halftime—I'd be just pissed as hell—and then by the time the third quarter is over, I've got 16 or 17 rebounds. Those are the best games. Those are the games where it hurts and then you rise above it. **I'm always looking for the pain** that's going to get my mind back to where it needs to be. I'm no good working from a comfort zone. I need pain. **I love pain.**

When I get 11 rebounds, I feel like shit. I don't feel like playing anymore. I really don't, because I'm not contributing to the team. I'm not doing what I get paid to do, and I'm not giving the team what it needs.

And you know what? **Eleven rebounds is a perfect game for a lot of these guys**

now. These guys now make a big deal out of a double-double. You get 11 points and 10 rebounds and you're a fucking hero.

At Southeastern Oklahoma I'd get 14 rebounds and there'd be all these people standing over me saying, "**What the hell is wrong with you?**" Fourteen is a phenomenal game for a lot of people. They'll hang that on the wall. But people expect me to get 18 or 19 rebounds every night—and I've done that over the last four years.

The way I see it, the minute you're satisfied with 14 rebounds, you're not far away from being satisfied with 11 or 10. If you get there, then you're **just like the rest** of these guys in the league.

Maybe **the strangest thing that ever happened to me** on a basketball court came at the Pontiac Silverdome in my third year with the Pistons. The ball was heading out of bounds and I went for it—like I always do—and landed in the stands. It was a wild, crazy dive, but I've done it a thousand times. The problem was, **I landed on this poor lady** and **knocked a few of her teeth out.**

She saw this as a chance to get some money. She was sitting in the front row, and she said she had never been to a game before and didn't know what to expect. She took me to court, and I had to pay her $60,000 because the judge ruled I was **reckless and out of line.** This was just basic basketball stuff—a guy diving for a loose ball. But it cost me $60,000. I found out she not only got her teeth fixed but got a whole new denture plate too. I think it's another example of somebody taking advantage of a situation.

This one, though—this was a new one. Even for me. It was probably a new one for the whole sports world.

All that **CRAZY SHIT** I do on the court keeps me interested. I try to find new ways to make this game a lot sexier. I'm trying to find new ways to make this game more attractive, even though it's already attractive. I want every person to leave that arena and say, **"God, did you see what he did today?"**

It's just like music; it's only good when you feel it. And I'm making you feel it. Very rarely do I feel somebody's emotions when I'm watching a game. **MAGIC JOHNSON DID IT,** but in a different way than I do. He did it with a smile and a laugh, and I do it with intensity.

I don't feel anything when I watch Shaquille O'Neal play. He plays hard, and he cares about the game, but I don't feel anything coming off him. He's one of those guys who were created before he arrived. He's been created as this "Basketball Animal." He plays with abandon, and he plays to win. But **how much do you really want to win when you have as much money, attention, and fame as he does?** It's got to be hard to keep it all straight, especially at his age.

Look at what happened almost as soon as I put on the uniform in Chicago: they were talking about the intensity and excitement I bring to practice,

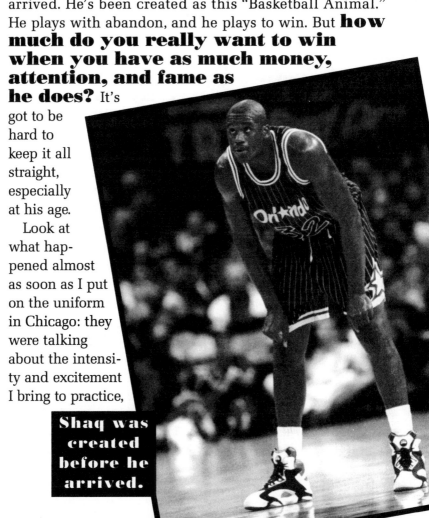

Shaq was created before he arrived.

how that was going to make players like Luc Longley better right away.

Luc got into a fight with Chris Webber of the Bullets early in the preseason and it came back to me. The Chicago papers and the people on the radio were talking about how I was making my presence felt by bringing out the toughness in Luc Longley. That was fine, but **I WASN'T THE ONE FIGHTING.** I was one of the guys trying to break it up.

You look at the way I act and play on the court, and you might come away thinking I fight all the time. You might think I get into fights in bars and on the street and wherever I am. It isn't like that, though. I'm cool. I can take a lot of crap before I get around to fighting. It's like those days in Oklahoma, when people were calling me **NIGGER** and telling me to **go back to Africa.** If I didn't take that step then, I'm sure as hell not going to now.

Besides, **most guys are scared** to fight me, because they think I'm all crazy. They don't know what I might do. They look at me like, "Okay, let's just go about our business here."

A lot of guys are *afraid to piss me off.* The only time I had a real knockdown fight was during my rookie year in Boston, and those fans never let me forget it. Everybody was in on that one, and it started with Bill Laimbeer and Robert Parish in the middle and went from there. I got into it with Parish, and I got into it with Danny Ainge, and before long guys were everywhere. I didn't really know who was coming at me and who was trying to break it up. I was throwing punches and getting restrained at the same time. They'd throw me out of the way and I'd come back and fight again. I got tossed out of the game, and I went away kicking and screaming. I've tried to forget about that fight and let it fall into the black hole.

Most of the time I do my fighting by saying, **"I'LL KICK YOUR ASS IN THE GAME."** Then, when the game's over, you know I won the war. That's the fight: when the guy has to go back over to the bench, after he gets yanked from a game, and say, **"YEAH, my ASS has been *BEATEN*."**

When you look at what I contribute on the court, what does it matter if I'm a little late to shooting practice? Who cares about that? I'm not going to go out there and shoot fifteen times a game, like most of these other guys. If I do get shots, they're going to be right under the basket, so what the hell? Why can't they cool a little?

The perfect coach would tell me, "It's all right to be late for practice every once in a while, but I expect you to bust your ass while you're here." That's the way it should be. That's Chuck Daly right there.

A coach should have that muscle to fine you. Of course he should, but I wouldn't fine a player if he was late and had a great excuse. I can't tolerate it when a guy's late, and then he makes it worse by not practicing hard. It would be different then. **I work my ass off** in practice every day. How many other guys can say the same thing? Not many.

In San Antonio I didn't get credit for that. They said, "He's late. He's late." But how many days am I late for practice? Almost never, and when I am it's one, two minutes late. My last year with the Spurs, **I was late to practice one time.** I was late once and I missed once. But the guys on the team were like little kids, watching the clock. I was early to practice almost every day, but I was always outside the gym, sitting in my truck listening to Pearl Jam, getting my mind right.

Everybody knows about the time I did this bad thing or that bad thing. I did something to John Stockton, or I did something to Karl Malone, or I did something to Scottie Pippen. What they don't know is that it's all a big psych job.

Everything I do out there is a psych. I'm trying to get into your head. I don't cuss you out. I don't sit there and make you feel like shit. I don't talk garbage. **You're going to feel like shit enough after I beat your ass, so I don't need to**

tell you about it. You know inside, and you know that I know. That's all that matters.

The trash talk is a waste of time. Those guys who do that are trying to boost themselves up. They're trying to make themselves bigger and badder than they already are. They're doing it for themselves, and I don't need that. They have to make sure they are somebody. What's the point of that?

Everybody's talking trash these days, so why not keep quiet? There's more impact if you burn somebody with your eyes, look straight into him and let him know with just a look. The talk gets in the way. I don't need to tell you what I'm doing to you. If a guy goes out of the game and looks over at me, Lord knows he's thinking, **What the hell can I do to stop this guy**—*this guy who's not even scoring a* basket? *He's dominating the game, and* **he's not even thinking about shooting.** That plays with their minds. They're thinking, What can I do? Hold him? That doesn't work; he just goes around me.

EVERYBODY wants to stop **DENNIS RODMAN.** That was true when I was in Detroit, and it became more true in San Antonio. When I got traded to Chicago, to play with Jordan and Pippen, other teams' desire to stop Dennis Rodman went to another planet, bro. They all wanted to prove they could derail this train we put together.

There are three players in history who have won more than one rebounding title in each conference: Wilt Chamberlain, Moses Malone, and me.

I'm not big enough to lead the league in rebounding all these years. There are only a couple guys you can compare me with. Charles Barkley did it—once. Michael Cage did it—once. But those guys are still bigger than me: Charles is six six and 250; Cage is six nine and 240. They're more powerful than me, stronger than me. I use basically what other guys are lacking. They've got all the power, all the strength, they've got the desire. I fill in the things they don't have, and **that's why it's such a mental challenge when you play against me.**

I work my body to stay in shape for the pounding I take under the boards. I only weigh 220, so I have to do something to keep from being tossed around by all the guys who weigh 250 and more. I train hard, but I don't try to get too big.

My game depends on flexibility and agility. I want to stay toned so my muscles don't get all bunched up to where I don't feel light and agile. I work out before games and after games—and the same goes for practices. I have to do that to stay fresh and competitive.

It's hard to explain to people how I can dominate a game with my rebounding. It's hard for someone to believe you can change a game around just because you want it so damned bad.

My friend Jack Haley has played with Magic Johnson and Michael Jordan, and he says the things I do on the court amaze him as much as what those guys do. Jack always says, "I could just stand and watch you, bro, because **nobody does what you do.**"

There are players who jump higher and have longer arms, but I do the things they aren't willing to do. They aren't going to stand under the basket, tipping the ball over and over, waiting for everybody to clear out so they can be there by themselves, just them and the ball. They aren't going to do that because it's too much work. They don't want to leave all their energy down there, because their thing is to go the other way and try to score. They also know **I'm the only one out there willing to work** like that, so they might as well jump a couple times and head back downcourt.

The way they look at it, they'll trade that rebound for a chance to get a dunk on *SportsCenter* that night.

I'm not finished crafting this art form, either. I can take rebounds to a new level. It's not just statistics that are important, it's **the flair** and **the style.** The next step for me is to expand on the style. The way I rebound is not like anybody else. When I rebound, it's like, "Wow." People notice it. I'm up in the air with the ball at my chest, and my legs are sticking out every which way. **THE BALL'S ALL MINE.**

I'm starting to see players trying to copy what I do. I'm flattered the players acknowledge the fact that I have a gift that other players want to emulate, just like they want to emulate the Michael Jordan dunks. I want to do for rebounds what Michael did for dunks.

The league doesn't appreciate what I've done for rebounding. They can't bring themselves to give me the credit I deserve for my accomplishments. The people I play against appreciate it, though. They know. They understand, because they can't believe I can do the things I do. They watch it and marvel at it.

Rebounding was never seen as a marketable skill in the NBA. They fill their commercials with dunks and last-second shots and Michael Jordan doing the things he does. I think the marketing people are beginning to see the beauty of rebounding now. **They're going to have to see it, because I keep hanging around.** The older I get, the better I get.

Most guys, are saying, "Yeah, did you see me score 25 points? Did you see me make that move?" That's all they care about. You aren't going to see me doing that. What kind of moves am I going to make on a rebound?

People say, "What are you talking about? **You can't score 20 points.**" Bullshit. I can score 20 points if I want to, but that's not my desire. My desire isn't to score 20 points, or outscore the guy I'm going against and say, "I beat his ass; he only had eighteen. Who cares if we lost?" I'm out there to be a piece of the puzzle, to go out there and beat the other basketball team.

The other side of my rebounding is my free-throw shooting. I can't begin to describe the amount of crap I've taken for being **a lousy free-throw shooter.** For me free-throw shooting is like a nasty chore, something I don't want to do. It's like *I'm scared to shoot the ball.* In 1994–95 it was my highest percentage of my career—68 percent. Even that's not very good, but it beats what I did in 1989, when I shot 37 percent from the line over 15 games. **It's hard to be that bad, bro.**

But I can shoot free throws if I want to. There's something holding me back. It's like, **I've got to go,** I've got to be moving, and standing there on that free-throw line, with everything around me stopped, doesn't work for me. That's why **I take the thing and just shoot it.** No messing around, no form or anything. You see me sometimes and I look around and look around, not even dribbling the ball, and then I just shoot the thing. Sometimes my feet are moving when I'm shooting, and sometimes **I'm not even sure I'm looking at the basket.** I just **don't want to be up there;** I want the game to start moving again.

Reporters come up to me, coaches come up to me, they say, "You're not a very good free-throw shooter. You can't shoot free throws." But look around this league. Not many people are great free-throw shooters. I think it's more the way I approach it that bothers people.

One thing people overlook, though: **WHEN I NEED TO MAKE 'EM, I MAKE 'EM.** When the game's on the line, believe me—I'm going to make 'em. That's when I take my time and actually put some form into it. I can't tell you the number of times it's happened, but it's been quite a few.

If I could get my free-throw shooting up to 75 or 80 percent, then my scoring average would go up to at least double figures. Then I could walk around like all these other superstars, talking about all my double-doubles. That alone is a good reason not to worry about free-throw shooting.

Someday I might start scoring, though. **Wouldn't that blow everybody's mind?** What would happen if all of a sudden I was averaging 15 points a game and 18 rebounds—would they make me the MVP of the league? No, they'd probably call me **MOST IMPROVED.**

If I did that, it would really mess with their heads. They'd wonder, "Man, what's he gonna do next? He's full of surprises."

Everyone is so crazy over scoring, and that's part of why I'm not really interested in doing it. I could average 15 points a game if I wanted to. I could score 8 to 10 points a game on offensive rebounds alone. So averaging 14 or 15 a game wouldn't be that hard. I could get 4 hoops a game on tips. Watch the way I get my hands on the ball and you'll see that would be real easy. The thing is, though, it wouldn't be the thing that would help the team the most.

The effect I'm having in this league is easy to see. It's right there in every game I play: guys are trying to **hold Dennis Rodman, frustrate Dennis Rodman,** get him out of his game.

Denver is a team that has tried to do some unusual things with me. They put somebody out there to face-guard me the whole damned game when I was with San Antonio. Every time we played them, here's this damn guy with his hand in my face. I don't remember who the hell the guy was—I'm not real good with names of other players. They had one guy face-guarding me, and another guy guarding me on the other side. You'd think I'd be a guy they'd leave alone, because I'm no threat to score. But here's Denver, practically **double-teaming a guy who doesn't even want the ball.** And I still averaged 22 rebounds against them.

When teams try to trick me or bully me or hold me, I get frustrated. In that way what they're doing might work. But what's bad about it for the other team is, that frustration energizes me more. I'm so happy this is happening. **I want to be pushed around and hit and kneed.** The more blood, the better.

I have a psychological edge going into every game. The guy on the other side looks over at me and thinks, *God, this guy is* **so crazy, so wild,** *that I don't know what he's up to. He won't talk to anybody. He won't look at anybody.* **What's going on in that mind?**

I think that's what happened to Scottie Pippen in the 1991 play-offs. I was all over him that series, and I got fined for it—$5,000 worth—when I pushed him into the stands. After that he got a migraine headache and sat out a game. I think he probably did have a migraine, but I think I might have had a hand in giving it to him.

People don't know how to take me. You talk to coaches—except for Chuck Daly—and other players, and **THEY DON'T KNOW HOW TO REACH ME.** That's the way I like it. I don't want people in the game of basketball around me. I've built up this force field around myself, this mystery, and I don't want to lose that.

After I'd been with the Bulls for a few weeks, Scottie Pippen was asked by *Sports Illustrated* whether he'd had a conversation with me. Scottie said, **"No, I have not had a conversation with Dennis. I've never had a conversation with Dennis in my life, so I don't think it's anything new now."**

That's all part of my edge. If other players started to get to know me, they might find out I'm not the same guy they think I am. Then they might start to think they can contain me on the court. I'm not going to give them that opening.

You're going to have to **find a way to stop me on your own, BRO,** and nobody's found it yet.

Not many guys have been through what I've been through. If you've been told from the time you're thirteen that you're going to the NBA, you might not be as strong mentally as I am. I had to work my ass off and **CLIMB THROUGH A LOT OF SHIT**—remember that tunnel?—to get here. I know how important the mind is.

Some coaches will have a guy designated to come in and try to hurt Dennis Rodman. You know what I do? I say, "Okay, great—I accept this challenge. Try to hurt me." If you're going to hurt me, great, but you've got to make sure you put somebody in there that's a lot crazier, a lot wilder, and a lot more bizarre than I am. That's the only way it's going to work, and I don't know who that guy is. And you know what? **I'm not sure that guy exists.**

seven

True Colors

Race, On and Off the Court

When you talk about race in basketball, the whole thing is simple: **a black player knows he can** go out on the court and **kick a white player's ass.** He can beat him, and he knows it. It's that simple, and it shouldn't surprise anyone. The black player feels it every time. He knows it from the inside.

It doesn't always happen that way, though. John Stockton can take any point guard in the league. Danny Ainge was one of the toughest players around. Larry Bird was in a different class altogether. But what I'm talking about is attitude, and the black player has been conditioned to think **HE CAN TAKE THE WHITE GUY WHENEVER HE NEEDS TO.**

Black athletes look at their sport as more of a war than a white athlete does. The black athlete, especially in basketball, is out there to win that war every time. The way I see it, the black athlete has his whole reputation at stake every time he takes the floor.

129

The reason, I think, is that **sports are more important to the black athlete.** They always have been. There are exceptions, but for the most part white kids growing up have more opportunities. A black guy who grows up in the projects, like I did, doesn't have that many opportunities. The worlds are different.

The white athlete has so many more areas open for achievement. The white guy can go into any sort of business. He can get a summer job easier. He goes to better schools. He has a better chance of getting through high school and into a college. When it comes to sports, a lot of white guys can take it or leave it. They'll play, but they won't be thinking they're going to make a career out of it.

Black people also have the whole world open to them, but a lot of times they can't see it. Their schools might be lousy, their teachers might not care, their parents might not be around. The black guy from a poor background thinks sports first, everything else second. He's been taught from television and advertisements that sports is the quickest way to the top. He sees *two ways out of poverty:* SPORTS *or* DRUGS. It may not be right, but that's the way it is. The white guy from the suburbs doesn't have the same motivation to succeed in sports.

From a young age the competition is greater and rougher for the black athlete. From the time you're playing on the playground or in the street, you feel how hard it is. GUYS ARE OUT FOR BLOOD.

I also believe **black people have to play harder and better** to be accepted. They have to achieve and then overachieve. It's not as true in basketball, but in a lot of sports, society won't accept a black athlete unless he's great. **A white quarterback can be average and still have a job,** but the only black quarterbacks who get a chance are the stars. The ones who aren't stars, who are just average guys, get switched to wide receiver or defensive back.

If you see a black hockey player, it's like a miracle. Black people don't grow up with hockey, so if a black guy wants to play hockey, he's got to get the chance first, then he's got to be phenomenal. If he isn't, he won't even get the chance to start out in the sport.

Blacks dominate basketball almost as much as whites dominate hockey. I don't believe in the science talk of genetics and all that. I think black dominance in basketball has more to do with **BLACK GUYS WANTING IT**—and needing it—more than the white guy.

When I talk about race, I have to go right to the end of my rookie year, when **I made those comments about Larry Bird** after the Celtics beat us in the Eastern Conference Finals.

It was a tough series, and we lost the seventh game, 117–114, in Boston. Afterward, there was so much hurt in that locker room that you could almost feel it. We thought **we were the better team**, and **we were pissed as hell** at the way the fans in the Boston Garden had treated us. They yelled down at us the whole series, saying anything they felt like. They were yelling about guys' mothers, about their girlfriends and wives—and about basketball. It was the toughest crowd I'd ever faced, and it made what I went through when we played against the Bulls in Chicago seem like nothing.

I guarded Bird in that series, and afterward that was all anyone wanted to talk about. I wasn't in the mood to say the right things, so I just started talking. I said whatever came to mind, whatever I thought could make me feel better and maybe **get back at those fans.**

When they asked me about Bird, I said, "Larry Bird is overrated in a lot of areas. I don't think he's the greatest player. **HE'S WAY OVERRATED.** Why does he get so much publicity? **Because he's white.** You never hear about a black player being the greatest."

Isiah Thomas was sitting next to me, and he looked up and agreed. He said if Bird was black, "he'd be just another good guy."

A lot of people, mostly black people, thought it was true. Maybe it still is true, in some ways, today. But I was sitting there—frustrated, hot, pissed off—talking without thinking. I wanted to turn some of my hurt back on someone else, and Larry was the guy who got in the way. He was the best person to get on if you wanted to get back at the fans, because he was such a god there. None of that comes out in the newspaper, though: the way I said it, **I LOOKED LIKE A RACIST AND A SORE LOSER.**

I've got to give Larry Bird his due: he was a great player. He knew the game and he was smart. Those are the important things. It's not about black and white. It's about playing basketball, and the man could do that.

If I had thought about what I was going to say, I would have said it differently. I would have kept race out of it. I should have said, "Larry Bird is a great player, but he gets a lot of attention because he's in Boston, a place that hasn't had a dominant player in a long time. Bird

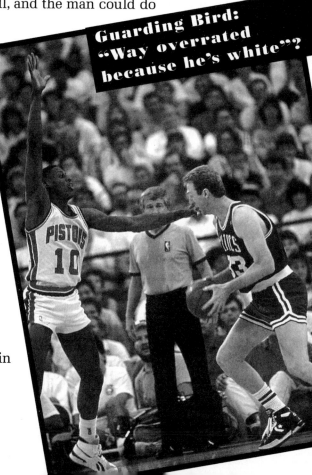

Guarding Bird: "Way overrated because he's white"?

gets a lot more attention because of where he plays."

I got hate mail after that. Tons of it. It was like I had burned the flag or something. A lot of people had never heard of me before this, because I didn't play all that much my rookie year. What a great way to get people to know your name. People were calling me a racist while I was sitting in Bokchito with the Riches, all of them white. At the time I was engaged to Annie, who is white. It didn't make a lot of sense when you put my words up against my life.

I never said anything to Bird after that. He and Isiah had a little press conference in Boston to smooth everything over. They sat there on a podium and Isiah said everything was taken the wrong way. Larry sat there and nodded, said there were no hard feelings. I went back to Oklahoma and went on with my life. **I started the damn thing, and then the stars had to clean it up.**

Bird never said anything to me about it, though. I guarded him all the time when we played back then, and he talked a lot—just never about that. He was one of the biggest trash-talkers I've ever been around. He'd run around after scoring a basket and say, **"Who's guardin' me? Nobody's guardin' me."** Then he'd look at me and say, **"You're supposed to be guardin' me?"** He went on like that the whole game sometimes.

That was back in my small-forward days, back when I was guarding all the big scorers. It was very difficult to put a rookie in that situation, to send me out there in the conference finals to guard Larry Bird. But I lived for that kind of thing, and Chuck Daly believed in me. I respected Bird, but I got to the point where **I DIDN'T GIVE A DAMN WHO HE WAS.** I was in there to be physical with him, to **bounce him around a little.** I was also supposed to outquick him—he was probably the slowest guy in the league. I couldn't outthink him, though, because he already had the game in his mind. He had prepared the game exactly as he wanted it.

Dennis Rodman

In that series I'd said to myself, "I'll go out there and do my job the best I can." They got the last word, though; they were the ones who went on to the Finals. I ended up sitting in the locker room, saying something I shouldn't have said.

I learned something from that: The issue of race is different inside sports than it is outside.

The locker room is probably one of the few places in America where black and white come together and deal with each other on a daily basis. Sure, black and white people work together in office buildings or construction sites, but they're not traveling together and practically living together like we do. I think the rest of society could learn something on race relations by using athletes as an example.

It's all out in the open when guys talk about race in the locker room. I can joke with Jack Haley, who is white, or black guys can joke with other black guys. It doesn't get complicated until society gets involved. If a white guy is around a black guy enough, he can call the black guy a nigger and everybody understands it's playful. But if you put it out there in society, with everybody looking at it and judging it, the rules are different.

There's no bullshit among teammates. In Detroit, Bill Laimbeer played the white-men-can't-jump role on our team. He knew he couldn't jump, and everybody else knew it. We could joke about it, call it **white man's disease,** and you knew he was going to take it the right way. You also knew he did enough good things on the court that he could make up for not being able to jump.

And if you find a black player who can't jump, the white guys love it. Everybody's on the guy, telling him how black men can't jump.

This is coming from somebody who doesn't see skin color. I'm color neutral. I'm black, but **MY FRIENDS JOKE ABOUT ME BEING A "WHITE" BLACK MAN.** Most of my close friends are white, and

I go out with white women. I don't think about color. I try to go beyond that.

The problem is, some people won't let you go beyond it. If you're black and a high-profile athlete, you're all of a sudden under pressure to be a **spokesman for the race.** It comes with the territory. Sometimes I think: *Fuck the race and the people, I'm going to be honest with myself.* That way, people—no matter what color—can make their own judgments about me.

Everyone has a different experience. Everyone has a different story. When it comes to attitudes about race, my experiences are different than anybody else's. I've been through some weird shit when it comes to race, and I've had a lot of chances to figure out where I stand on race issues. I've been a victim of racism, and I've been criticized for being too white.

There were times when race confused me. **There were many times I thought I wanted to be white.** I wasn't accepted in the black community when I was growing up. I was teased and picked on for my looks, and this was where I was supposed to feel comfortable. When I got to college in Oklahoma, I found out **I didn't fit into a white community** either. I wondered if I would ever fit in as long as my skin was black.

I can remember when I was a little kid in Dallas during the civil-rights marches, in the mid- to late sixties. There was a lot of hatred toward white people in my neighborhood. In 1968, after Martin Luther King was killed, **I WATCHED THESE MEN BEAT A WHITE MAN TO DEATH** on the streets of the Oak Cliff projects. They just stomped him and hit him on the sidewalk, until he didn't move anymore. I was seven years old at the time, and I didn't think much of it. We all knew what happened when white people came in there—they were beaten up or they had rocks and bottles thrown at their cars. That's the way it was. It wasn't right, but when you're young you just accept things without wondering about them.

When I was in college, my color followed me everywhere. Before I became known as a basketball player, **I was called "NIGGER" all the time.** I'm sure those people still called me that after I brought some attention to the school because of basketball, but they just did it behind my back and under their breath. It was a tough place for me, and I'd get pissed off. When I first got there, I didn't know how to handle that type of thing, so the only way I could think to deal was to hurt somebody.

I didn't, because I had someone—Bryne or James Rich—there to make sure I didn't do anything stupid. But there were times, though—there were times when I was close to going off. I don't know where I would have stopped, either.

This was Durant, Oklahoma—population six thousand—and if they didn't like to see you walking around campus, **IMAGINE WHAT THEY THOUGHT OF A BIG BLACK MAN DATING WHITE GIRLS** from the community. You can probably figure it out.

They don't see many black people to begin with in rural Oklahoma. And of the ones they do see, they don't want to see them dating their daughters. I remember one father in particular who wanted my ass for dating his daughter during my junior year at Southeastern Oklahoma. We usually tried to go out without her parents knowing, and one time she told me to come over because her parents were going to be gone for a few hours.

It turned out like a bad movie: They came home early and **FOUND ME IN THE BEDROOM WITH THEIR DAUGHTER.** I heard them coming, so I gathered up my clothes and started for the back door. **Her father grabbed a rifle and came after me** with it; he shot at me as I ran out the back door and down the block. Even though I grew up in the projects, this was the first time somebody had taken a shot at me, and I was scared.

This showed me something about the girl too. She knew how her father felt about me, but she took the chance. She was the one who pursued me too. She knew the risks, and even though I was the one getting shot at, she was going to hear about it too.

There are so many things that could have kept me from being where I am. I go back to the times when people would be telling me to go back to Africa, and the only thing I could think to do was to use the gun, or that shovel. Instead, I learned to roll with things, and I realized that **some people want to have controversy between the races.** The only way they know how to deal with people is to make them out to be the enemy, or less than human. I went through a lot of racial garbage, but I came away with a better understanding. I wasn't screwed up by it; I learned from it.

There's a lot of hatred in the world, and it isn't all in one place.

Everything I went through added up to something, though; it made me accept anything that comes my way. Most people coming from my background aren't as fortunate, to have a family like the Riches come in and teach you how to deal with things you're going to have to face the rest of your life.

I think this: If you put one hundred black people and one hundred white people in a neighborhood and have them grow up together from childhood, they're going to think of each other as one. They won't draw lines to separate themselves. They won't see it as black and white. It would be like *one big locker room,* where people aren't afraid to say whatever they want, knowing it won't be taken the wrong way.

BLACK CULTURE is something I **don't relate to** much at all. It seems people look at black culture nowadays as nothing more than gangsta rap. If you don't buy into that, you don't buy into black culture.

I understand what the rappers are talking about. I

understand because I lived it. I've been there, and I go back. I saw it every day in Oak Cliff. But **I THINK RAP IS LESS ABOUT EDUCATING PEOPLE** about the problems of the black community and **MORE ABOUT MAKING MONEY.** They're exploiting a situation. They're taking advantage of people's pain, making money off their problems.

I don't think they're feeling what they're singing. I think they're trying to decide what is going to sell best, not only among black kids but among white kids.

I do think there is a good side to rap, though. It gives people a sense of what black people went through and are still going through. You see **all these white kids** walking around malls or wherever listening to rap and **dressing and talking like black kids?** Their parents probably don't like it, but maybe they're going to grow up with a better understanding of black people. I look at those white kids and it looks to me like they want to be black. It makes me think back to times when **I WANTED TO BE WHITE** because I didn't feel a part of the black community where I grew up, and I didn't feel a part of the white community in Oklahoma.

Sometimes I think rappers are trying to say, "Here's a tour of the projects." They're trying to put a bunch of white people and black people who don't live in these areas on a bus tour of the projects. They're saying, **"Here, bro, take a look for yourself."**

More than anything I think they're selling out their neighborhoods. There are certain things I do, I admit, that make me feel like shit. Sometimes **I'll do a commercial or an endorsement and think, I don't believe in this. Why am I doing it?** I'll be down on myself, thinking all I'm doing is selling out.

Those things bother me, and that's **why I relate to PEARL JAM so much.** I relate to them— and get along with them—better than the guys playing rap or the guys playing in the NBA. I relate to them because they are so totally true to their craft, just like I'm true to my craft.

In 1993 Pearl Jam's bass player told the other guys in the band he wanted to meet me. He told Eddie Vedder and the other guys that I was the same on the basketball court as they are onstage. They could see I believe in what they believed in.

I liked their music before I met them, because it hit me at home. I felt it. If you really listen to them, you can tell the difference between them and any other band right away. The connection between me as a basketball player and them as a band comes from **the emotion we both show when we perform.** It's easy to show emotion, but the key is to get other people to feel it.

When it comes to that, there's no band like Pearl Jam, and there's no singer like Eddie Vedder. In basketball there's nobody like me. I might play the same game every night, but it's always a different performance. You always walk away knowing you've seen something new. It's basketball, but it's something more. That's the same with Eddie Vedder; he might be singing the same songs every appearance, but each time he makes you feel something different. You could watch them in concert ten times and never come away with the same feelings.

Music plays a big part in my life; it helps me get ready for games and practices, and it helps me get my mind straight. Almost always I listen to Pearl Jam. You listen to them and you know what they're going through, and what life is all about. You can see it in their faces, just like you can see it in my face when I'm out on the court.

I was supposed to go on tour with them in the summer of 1995, but that got canceled when Eddie got sick and they postponed their tour. I've got a standing invitation to play the drums and sing, but I don't think I'm ready for that yet. I still have to work on my vocal cords before I take the stage.

During the summer I lived in ultra-conservative Orange County, I was driving through the town of La Habra in my black Ferrari. I was with my friend and business manager, Dwight Manley. He and I were just going for something to eat, and from the back I see a cop, flashing his lights, telling me to pull over.

He came over to the side of the car and I said, "What I do, man? I wasn't speeding." He looked at me like a real hard-ass and said, **"GET OUT OF THE CAR and I'LL SHOW YOU."**

We walked to the back of the car and he tried to tell me the registration was expired. I said, "Bro, those are Texas license plates. The registration's on the front window."

He looked at me kind of funny, then asked me for my ID. I gave him my license, he looked at my name, and everything changed.

He started saying shit like "Oh, man, nice car. I really like your style. Sorry for the trouble."

I guess he recognized my name, but he didn't recognize me, which is kind of hard to believe. My hair was fuchsia, but I had a baseball cap on over it.

But this guy was typical of the bullshit that comes out of this society. He sees a **BLACK DUDE IN A NICE CAR,** and he figures there must be something wrong. Probably a drug dealer, right? Going through that conservative-ass town, he didn't know what to think. Maybe he thought **we were invading, in our Ferraris.**

That happens to me pretty often, and I know it happens to other athletes. Everything's cool after they find out who I am. **The POLICE IN DALLAS used to stop my mother all the time** when she was driving the Mercedes I gave her. It got to the point where she got rid of the car because she was tired of being stopped all the time. The cops don't believe a black woman could have a big, nice car. She got rid of it because they were making her feel like a criminal for driving a nice car.

I used to think all that would change once I made it to the NBA and established myself, but it hasn't. I'm making it now, but I'm very uncomfortable going into a fancy restaurant.

PEOPLE ARE THREATENED BY ME.

Rich whites, rich blacks, it doesn't matter. Both sides are going to think I'm a threat because of the way I look. If I wasn't who I am, I wouldn't be allowed into nice restaurants—or even movie theaters—because they would automatically think I was a gang-banger. One look at me with my tattoos, my hair and my jewelry, and that's all they would consider. People accept me now only because I have money and some fame. I'm not going to get all carried away over that, and start thinking I'm accepted by these people, because I know better. I'm not.

I go out with WHITE WOMEN.

This makes a lot of people unhappy, mostly black women.

I've had people come up to me and say, **"Why don't you date a black woman?"** I don't really have an answer for that, because I don't think I'm going out of my way to avoid black women. It's just kind of the way it works out.

Black men with white women: it's a big issue these days. Black women think black men who become successful turn their back on them and take up with white women. I guess they could say I fall into that category. **My EX-WIFE is white. MADONNA is white. All my STEADY GIRLFRIENDS have been white.**

My story is a little different, because I wasn't the one turning my back on anyone. It worked the exact opposite with me, bro. **Black women didn't accept me** when I was younger. I wasn't attractive. I didn't have money or fancy clothes. I wasn't whatever it was they wanted.

Now, though, I'm okay. Now that I have some money and some fame, the story has changed. Some of those same black women who wouldn't talk to me years ago were rushing through the doors of my mother's house, asking, **"Where's your son? How's your son doing?"**

It was amazing, but once I made the NBA they started to get concerned about how I was doing.

Back before I was somebody, black women in the neighborhood wanted cars, clothes, and money. You had to look good, too, and I didn't have any of that. **I'M STILL NOT THE BEST-LOOKING GUY IN THE WORLD,** but they see the glamour and the money and they're on the bandwagon, wondering why I date white women.

I think black women are more dominant than white women. Black women are confident with themselves. They've had to run the family in a lot of cases because the man isn't around, and they learn to be strong.

White women are confident, but I think they're more concerned with their looks and how they come across to other people. To some extent every person is concerned about looks, no matter the color, but I think it's more obvious with white men and women. Black people are more laid-back and don't-give-a-damn, just go out there and do your thing.

A lot of white women who date black men say the black men treat them better than white men do. That's not always true, but I think a white woman can think **dating a black man is the best thing in the world** because it's something new. It's not her same culture, so she's learning something and trying to be a part of it. That can be exciting, and if a black man treats her nicely, she thinks she's got everything.

The other thing, of course, is that white women get into relationships with black men because they think **the sex is going to be better.**

Some people say they date people from another race because they don't see color, and that's the way it is for me. I also think it's refreshing for a white woman to be with a black man; that adds something to the relationship. They feel they can do anything, or say anything, to a black man and not be judged for it. There's more openness, more of a feeling that you don't have to conform to everything society tells you.

It's very common in the NBA for black players to have white wives or girlfriends. It's more common, in general, for a black person with status to date white women.

It's back to that **DOUBLE STANDARD:** If you're a basketball player, a movie star, or an entertainer, it's more acceptable for you to cross racial boundaries. If you're just a normal, everyday person, people look at you like you're doing something wrong.

There have been many times, none of them recent, when *I sat back and wished I was white.* It's sort of complicated, because I didn't want to be white just because white people have advantages black people don't, and I didn't want to be white only so I could go into a place like Durant, Oklahoma, and be accepted.

I grew up in the projects, where everyone was black. But I feel I was abused within that culture. I wasn't accepted there. I was too SKINNY, too UGLY, too SOMETHING. These were supposed to be "my people," but they didn't treat me like I was one of theirs.

Growing up, I was picked on in school, picked on everywhere. It was hard, and I didn't know what I could do about it. It was just there, and I had to deal with it. I solved it by standing up and being my own man, not everybody else's idea of what I should be.

Before I got the fame and the money, I wasn't accepted by black people, and I wasn't accepted by most white people. I wasn't the right color for any situation I found myself in. I'm sure a lot of kids and young people go through that. They think like I did: **_I want to be the right color._**

When I got to Oklahoma, I decided to turn my back on everything I had left behind. My only chance at success was to look straight ahead and forget the stuff back on the streets. Then I met Bryne and his family, and all I wanted was to be accepted as his friend. I wanted to be white, because I wanted to be accepted. I wanted Bryne's mom to be able to go the fastest way home. I wanted the people in the cars, and the fathers of the white girls, to stop looking at me as nothing but a black man. **IF I WERE WHITE, _I thought I could be a little happier._**

I wanted to be white because I was black, and **BLACK WAS NEVER THE RIGHT COLOR.**

eight

Sex

Who, What, When, Where, and Why

Fifty percent of life in the NBA is **SEX. The other fifty percent is MONEY.**

Off the court that's how it breaks down: fifty money, fifty sex.

THE NBA IS THE PLACE FOR THE HOT WOMEN. If you want your choice of women, this is the place for it. You **DON'T GO TO FOOTBALL OR BASEBALL** or any other sport. Basketball is known for the women who hang around the games. Within sports this wasn't a secret, but it started getting more attention after Magic Johnson revealed that he was HIV positive. That put the focus on sex in the NBA, and the media started looking at how women consider basketball players the ultimate sex objects.

Every city in the league has a group of women who hang around the arenas and know where the players go after the games. They're pros, and a lot of them are sexy as hell.

Women love basketball players. They just adore basketball players. *THEY WANT TO FUCK BASKETBALL PLAYERS.*

I wasn't prepared for the sex part of the NBA when I

145

first got into the league. It wasn't even close, because there was nothing in my past to prepare me. I had to learn fast, though—everything hit at once.

I've learned to handle the status and the power that come with being an NBA player, but I didn't have a good feel for it at first. I went to Southeastern Oklahoma, a tiny NAIA school in the middle of nowhere, not North Carolina or Duke. I didn't sign many autographs in college, and when I got to the NBA I didn't know why people, all of a sudden, wanted my autograph.

Multiply that by a hundred times and you'll get what I thought of the whole sex scene in the NBA. If I couldn't understand why someone wanted my name on a piece of paper, **how was I going to understand why all these women wanted to SLEEP WITH ME?** If I'd gone to North Carolina or someplace like that, I would have been more prepared for what was out there in the NBA. I wasn't that fortunate, so I had to learn as I went along.

The last few years have turned me into the Madonna of the NBA, the Madonna of the sports world. I don't know how it's happened. I'm not the best-looking guy around, but **people want to FUCK DENNIS RODMAN.** It's true for **both *females* and *males*.**

This is the ultimate turnaround. When I was a kid, the girls made fun of me and didn't find me attractive at all. I was skinny and small and they thought I was funny-looking. Now, they all want me. **TOO MANY OF THEM WANT ME.**

I'm still not the most attractive person in the world, but I've overcome that by being the one with the most confidence, the most flamboyance. It's like I don't give a fuck, and girls like that. Not just girls—*people* like that.

Of course, a lot of times women want to sleep with a basketball player just because he's a basketball player. That happens more than anybody outside the sport could imagine. There are women out there who live their whole life around sleeping with athletes. They're the ones you have to watch out for, because a lot of them are always scheming to get money off somebody. It sounds harsh, but I've seen enough of it to know it's not bullshit. I've been through it.

It's like a big network out there, and these women find out where players are. They find out what hotels the teams stay in, and they go there and hang out in the hotel bars. **There's a whole underground in each NBA city;** the women find out the clubs guys like to go to, they know the hotels and they stick around after games trying to get a player's attention.

They're not dumb. They get a whole portfolio on a player. I've heard about **women who cut out the salaries of all the NBA players** when they're printed in the newspaper so they can decide who they want to go after. The get all the information they think is necessary, then **THEY TARGET SOMEBODY AND GO AFTER HIM.** It's pretty amazing how involved some of them get in the whole process.

There are certain girls throughout the league that everyone knows. They make their way from team to team, trying to rack up numbers and maybe find someone who will take care of them. Some players talk among themselves about these women, but I'm not much for that. That's treating someone like a piece of meat, and I don't think that's a good way to talk about someone. As a matter of fact, I'm not interested in the girls who are building up numbers of players they've slept with. I know the girls talk about players—**who's good in bed, who isn't**—but I don't want any part of that. Most of the time, I'm not hanging out where most of the players are, anyway.

But I've had girls tell me things about other players. That's pretty much an **automatic turnoff** for me. There's nothing worse than having a girl tell you something that happened when she was in bed with another player. Am I supposed to care? Am I supposed to tell somebody else? I wouldn't tell anybody that stuff, and I wouldn't name the players who were mentioned. Any girl who would do that is bad news right off the bat. You get involved with a woman like that and you might find yourself in a position you don't want to be in. She might decide to sue you just so she can get some money out of you. Sometimes those girls are desperate—they think this is the way to get money and status—and it's really sad.

When it comes to women and what they're after, **I CAN SEE THROUGH A LOT OF THE CRAP.** I've been on the other side, where they didn't care about me because I didn't look right or have enough money. Sometimes, when I'm approached by a girl somewhere, I call them on it. I can have some fun with that.

For instance, I was in a bar in Newport Beach the summer after my last year with the Spurs, and I'd had a few drinks, so I was pretty much saying whatever came to mind. This blond girl, probably about eighteen, came up to me all giggly and said, "I just love you, Dennis."

My hair was fuchsia at the time. I had my nose ring in, four earrings, tattoos showing—the whole thing.

I looked down at her real seriously and said, "You love me, huh?"

"Yeah, I do," she said.

"I'm standing here with pink hair, a ring in my nose, all these earrings—darling, **would you love me if I didn't play ball?**"

She looked at me like she was terrified, smiled a little and walked away. She thought I was just going to say, "thank-you" and shake her hand. She didn't know what the hell was wrong with me.

I **GOT A LATE START ON SEX.** I wasn't particularly attractive to girls when I was a teenager, and I got laid for the first time when I was twenty, by a prostitute in the projects. I think she did me and my friends for twenty bucks. But I never thought of my sex life in the NBA as trying to make up for lost time. That thought never occurred to me.

The first time I put on that Pistons uniform, I discovered something: **As long as I play ball, I can get any woman I want.** If you want to know the truth about it, there it is. If you've got money and the status that comes with playing in the NBA, you can get anybody you want. Money is power and power is money.

That first day I slipped on the uniform that said NBA on it, I told myself, "You are now in the NBA." I was thinking about it only in basketball terms, but I found out it goes beyond that. The uniform was the ticket to whoreville and fuckville and slutville. That was the ticket to any door in the world to be open to you. You don't need condoms or anything, just go in there and help yourself. Just go in there and wallow in somebody's bedroom.

Sex plays a very important part in my life. I admit that. I'm in a position where **I can have sex anytime I want sex,** so I can turn it on and off in my mind. That's the beauty of it. I'm in charge, I guess you could say. The truth is, I can call a girl and have her over here right now. Give me fifteen minutes and I'll have a gorgeous girl.

It's just out there, all of it. The whole world's an open door, and some guys lose their soul trying to knock down every one of those doors. You have to know what's out there, and then you have to visualize what you can get out of it. Who can I get? Is it going to be a good lay, and can I come back and get it again and have it be the same way?

An NBA team on the road is similar to a band on tour. Groupies hang around bands; groupies hang around basketball teams. In music you've got sex and drugs and money. In basketball you've got women and money.

Sports is very elegant. Basketball players are very elegant. You've got to have your own style and charisma.

You've got to have poise and sex appeal. If you have that, women and men look at you and say, "Damn, I want that."

I have that style, and a lot of guys want it but can't pull it off. Right now in the NBA I don't see anybody else really pulling it off. I see **a lot of guys who are trying to emulate the things that I do.** They're trying to add something to what they have, and more than anything, **IT'S FAKE.**

More players have tattoos than ever before. More players have earrings. More players are trying to appeal to the Generation X, grunge element. Those are things that have come naturally to me. I had a tattoo before it was cool, or accepted. I wore earrings and a nose ring and a navel ring, and most people in the league thought I was crazy. Now you look around and see more players trying to pull off that look, that aura.

I try to keep people guessing about me, but I think it's gotten almost out of control. In San Antonio they were having radio call-in polls, asking people what they thought I would do next. What's his next hair color? Will he be on time? Is he really going to paint his fingernails? It's like I became an obsession, just because I was different from what they were used to seeing from a professional athlete.

It amazes me every time I think about it: **Why do people care** so much about those things? I don't understand it, but as long as they do care, I'll keep them entertained.

I would never keep track of the number of women I've been with. That's a cheap thing, I think. I can't lie like Wilt Chamberlain. **WILT CHAMBERLAIN LIED OUT OF HIS ASS** and made some money. I don't want to sit around and try to count, or say how many women a week I average and all that. It's not a game. **There's no scoreboard in my bedroom.**

Wilt Chamberlain said he had twenty-thousand women.

Think about that. That's three or four women a day for fifteen to twenty years. I dare anybody to keep up that kind of pace. **WILT SHOULD OPEN HIS OWN FUCKING SPERM BANK** and be the richest man in the world. I just think **THAT WAS A BUNCH OF SHIT.**

Sexual performance is a major part of the NBA life. It becomes part of the underground knowledge of the girls who hang with players. If you make the decision to jump in bed with a girl, you've got to jump in there with the intention of being good. They expect that. If you're not good—if you're bad—then you at least have to *make sure you sound like you're good.* You have to make them believe you're having the time of your life.

Players look at sexual performance like their performance on the basketball court. You've got to be a performer. You've got to be an actor when you're having sex with women on the road. It's like you're giving this woman **a private performance,** and you have to give her **SOMETHING TO REMEMBER YOU BY.** If you're single, and you want to go out and sleep around, that's what you've got to be: an actor. If you're not, word gets around.

If a guy is just out there doing it for himself and not treating the women with respect, he'll have a harder time finding someone the next time around. These girls talk. The players can talk about the groupies in different cities—who to stay away from and who's cool—and the girls can tell the same about the players.

I've found that these women have a tendency to do whatever they can to be with someone who has money. It's tough on players, because **you can get sucked down in a big hurry.** If you don't know what's out there, like I didn't know when I first got into the league, you can be in big trouble. Once you get around and learn about these things—after you've been bitten a couple of times—it puts you in the position of distrusting everyone.

There was a girl in Atlanta that I hung around with

whenever I was in that city. She was **a cheer-leader for the Hawks,** and she was cool. We slept together quite a few times and had a pretty easy, low-key relationship for three or four years. She was just a friend, nothing serious—at least that's what I thought.

I didn't know this at the time, but she used to keep everything I ever gave to her in this box. I'm not talking about gifts or love letters. I'm talking about *anything*—a piece of paper I wrote a phone number on, a piece of note paper I tore into pieces because I was bored, a receipt from dinner. Anything.

There were letters in there from me that said, "If nothing comes out of this relationship, I still want to be friends. We'll always be friends."

It wasn't like, "You're my girlfriend and I want to spend the rest of my life with you." It wasn't like that, but the way she kept everything it was obvious that's what she thought of the relationship. If I gave her a little friendship card or something, it was in there. If I scribbled on something, it was in there.

Sometimes when I just want to be friends with a girl, she won't let me. I want to be able to just hang out on the road or wherever, but most women will take it as a love relationship. If it's not like that, in the end they get hurt. It doesn't matter if you express it up front and say you just want to be friends and not take it beyond that. They still don't understand. They think, **"Well, if I do you good enough in bed, it'll work out."**

As it turned out, that's where this Hawks cheerleader was heading. She sued me in early 1995 for $1.5 million. She claimed I gave her herpes and that I owed her that much money because of it.

First off, **I DON'T HAVE HERPES.** That, to me, was the beginning and the end of the case. In the end, the jury agreed with that and I won the case, but not before I had to take it through a full-blown trial, which cost me $225,000 in lawyers' fees. So I won, but I lost. **I GOT SCREWED.**

The name of the game for some women is to trick guys in the league into getting married, or into giving them whatever they want. If the player won't take the bait, they try some other way to get what they want. They just want to sleep with an athlete and then make the athlete pay for everything. In this life that's pretty much an everyday occurrence.

I should have known with her, probably, but I couldn't see it. I try to give a girl the benefit of the doubt, and it wasn't like this was a one-night stand. I never suspected that I was being set up. After she filed the suit, she thought she was going to settle out of court. She said, **"Okay, give me five hundred thousand and I'll forget it."** I said, **"For what? For me not giving you herpes?"**

That's crazy. That's why I took it to court. If I didn't think I was going to win, if I thought she had a case, I would have paid her off to make it go away and keep it out of the newspapers.

I think I won the case by going up there and testifying myself. I said, "If I did have herpes—and I don't—it's the responsibility of both parties if you decide not to use a condom. It was agreed on her part and on my part that we would not use a condom." It wasn't like I was trying to rape her or hide something from her.

She said I wouldn't let her look at me, that it was dark and I took a shower in the dark—all this crazy stuff that never happened.

The box she kept was brought into evidence too. This got everybody in the courtroom laughing, even the jury. How could a girl that I'm not even seeing seriously be that far out to keep all this crap? I could tell the jury was sitting there thinking, **Is this a frame-up or what? Is she trying to frame him for a million dollars?** I think the answer to that was yes, that's exactly what it was.

I don't know if I really trusted her. I don't really trust

anybody. If I want to hang out with a girl, that's great, but I'm not really trusting her. Girls take things too seriously. They say, "This guy's really nice to me. I think I want to see him more and more." Sometimes they can't see that it's just friendship.

I've had other lawsuits, not counting my divorce. One girl said **I was patting her on the ass,** another said **I was saying crazy stuff to her.** Then there was the women in Detroit who got $60,000 from me because I dove into the stands after a loose ball and knocked a couple of her teeth out. **I THINK I MUST LEAD THE LEAGUE IN WEIRD SHIT.**

After a while you know you're going to get this kind of craziness in this business—petty, stupid stuff—but it's still difficult. It's still hard to look at someone and realize they're living their life to get money from somebody.

If I was just some so-called "normal" person, they wouldn't care if I patted them on the ass or even walked up to them and kissed them. They'd slap me in the face and that would be the end of it. But they see somebody with money and stature, and they think, *Hey, he hit me, and I better get something out of it.* They make it a big deal—whether it's real or not.

When there's no money involved, it's different. **MONEY CHANGES EVERYTHING.** It makes people try to make something out of nothing. It gives them a chance to get something the easy way— something they wouldn't normally have.

People find it hard to believe that I could make as much money as I have the past six years and not have anything saved. They don't realize how much of my money's gone to lawyers. If I hadn't had to pay lawyers over the past five or six years, I think I'd have three or four million dollars in the bank right now. The divorce settlement alone will end up costing me something like $2 million.

When it comes to women, I hate to admit it, but the first thing I think is that *they're trying to get something from me.* That's always my first thought. All this stuff that has happened to me has made me think that way. Some groupies are fine as hell, very good looking, gorgeous. And some of them are smart. But the only direction some of them have is to sleep with athletes. They make it a goal to sleep with as many as they can, hoping they'll find one that will stick around and provide for them.

I didn't know much about this at first. Slowly but surely I started learning. When I was a rookie, there were guys whispering stuff in my ear, like, "Be careful out there, Dennis. Don't go for that." But you pretty much have to learn on your own. You make mistakes, then try not to make them again.

Coming out of college, I was innocent. I had no choice but to change, to become harder and more cynical.

I learned that it's easy to go fuck somebody. It's easy and it's available. You don't have to think about it, and it's fun. It's a great feeling—every guy's dream is to have women there for the taking, right? But at some point you've got to ask yourself, **"Am I doing the right thing? Am I actually doing the right thing by sleeping with this person I just met?"**

Sometimes I'll sleep with someone and right after it's the worst feeling in the world. I'll be lying there thinking, *Oh, shit. Damn, what did I do that for?* I'll feel like I used someone for sex, and that I cheapened myself in the process. That's not a good feeling.

I imagine I'll get married again. There will come a time when I'll want to settle down and check out of this rat race. But if I do get married again, there will have to be an understanding between the two of us. She will have to really understand my history, that I got into a bad situation with Annie—a situation I'll probably pay for the rest of my life. I'm not going to go through that again. I don't care how good-looking you are, or how fine you are, you're going to have to be totally straight up with me. You're going to have to be in it for the right reasons. You're going to have to be able to hang with me **if I end up back working at the airport.** You're going to have to be able to take me after I'm finished playing and the bright lights are turned off. You're going to have to be prepared for that, because that's the only way I can deal.

When it comes to sex, I think I've heard it all. The wildest thing I get is from married couples. They'll come up to me in a bar or after a game, and *the man will tell me he wants me to fuck his wife.* He wants me to do her while he watches. It's her fantasy, and the man's too.

The first time I got this proposition was in a club in Dallas. I couldn't believe it. I was blown away. Since then, it's happened many times—a bunch of times in a rest room, for some reason. The husband will follow me in there and ask me to do it. They actually want me to do this.

My response to them is simple: Why? Why do you think you want this?

They say, "My wife wants it."

I say, "Okay, so I guess that makes it all right?"

"My wife really likes you, and I'd like to see you fuck my wife."

I look at the guy and say, "Okay. You want to see me fuck your wife? I'd like to see the expression on your face if I ever *did* fuck your wife. How would you feel when your wife likes it? I think you'd be standing there saying, 'Oh, shit.' And then what if she comes up to me and says, **'I want to do it again, without my husband knowing about it'?"**

I can't do that. I would never do that. It's not a surprise to me anymore. At the beginning it was a shock. I was like, "What in the *hell*? God*damn*, that's crazy." Now it's just a part of my life. I'm accustomed to hearing the crazy shit, so **IT'S GOING TO TAKE MORE THAN THAT TO SHOCK ME.**

For some couples their dream is to have something like that—with a famous person—in their life. If you're really sexually active, maybe you dream about that. I think *every man dreams about having TWO WOMEN on him.* I think every man would enjoy that, *unless he's a priest.*

That's different than the guy who wants to watch me do his wife, but I think you've got people out there who wish they could have two guys and a girl. There is a part of society that is into stuff like that. I know it because I've seen it firsthand. Some of the times, the husband wants to watch me—that's his fantasy. Then other times the husband wants to participate too.

You've got a crazy mess out there, and there are people who are into some really wild stuff. I've been tossed into the middle of it because people see me as very sexual, and the time I was with Madonna made people believe **I'm the kind of person who would do anything at any time.**

There are people who want to explore every possibility. *That's why pornography is so popular.* People go out there and see that stuff and let it live in their soul. They can visualize it in those pictures, and they somehow get to believing that's what they want. Why do you have sex magazines? So you can go out and buy it and beat off, and hope someday it can happen to you. That's where a lot of it comes from. Some people are just bolder about asking for it. I guess they figure the worst thing that can happen is that I say no.

Don't get me wrong. I've bought my share of magazines. I've bought my share of movies. **I've had my share of lonely nights with Judy (my right hand) and Monique (my left hand).** I'm not going to deny that. I'm guilty of that as much as the next guy.

Some men, a lot of men, might think it's flattering to have a woman and a man come up and hit them with the proposition I've been hit with. I'm used to it, so I let it roll off, but it can be seen as an insult. **It's like I'm just this sex object,** something you can play with and experiment with. They act like **it doesn't matter what I**

want. They assume I want to do something like that, because of my reputation or my flamboyance. Some of them think I'm looking at their wives, checking them out, and so I'm interested enough to take them both on.

The way I look at it, if I do that, it means I'd do the same thing to my wife or my girlfriend. It means I'd want her to fuck one of my friends. I can't do that. I'm not like that.

Other players in the league get hit with this stuff, too, but I don't know what other players do about it. I don't talk to other guys or associate with them in that way. I just know **I've come to expect it. I've come to expect just about any-thing in this crazy world.**

I don't think the revelation that Magic Johnson has HIV changed anybody's mind when it comes to sex in the NBA. I don't think it changed attitudes or behavior. If you're in the NBA, you think you're invincible. You think you're bulletproof.

AIDS isn't much more than a pass-ing thought, something that happens to other people.

In the NBA you've got a little control, a little power, a lit-tle status in your hand. You've got the joystick for a short period of time. Your life is going to depend on how you operate that joystick and the way you control your army.

When it came out that Magic was infected with the virus, everybody was shocked. No one expected that from a big-name NBA star. No one believed it could happen.

I would never say anything bad about Magic—we're friends—but people shouldn't have been shocked that a superstar athlete came down with HIV. If someone else has AIDS, someone who is just a regular person and not a big-name star, nobody is shocked. When it's someone down the street or in your office building, people say, "It's an aggressive, terrible disease." People are sad, but they're not so shocked they stop their lives.

It's ridiculous how this world can protect an NBA player and somehow make him out to be a god at the same time. **We're supposed to be immune from things like AIDS? Come on.** And if we do come down with it, all we have to do is go on television and apologize, maybe say, "I can't believe this happened to me. I should have been more aware."

That's the truth too. **WE SHOULD BE MORE AWARE.** No question about it. But we as basketball players or athletes are no more innocent or guilty than any normal human being. Magic shouldn't have to apologize for getting a disease, like he let people down by getting sick. That doesn't make sense to me.

When the news first hit, there was all this publicity about the habits of professional athletes. There was a big push to have everybody start using condoms. Everyone wanted to know whether this would change the way athletes had sex.

For the first couple of weeks I think it made a difference. Guys were using condoms and maybe being a little more careful about who they slept with. But then it died down, and it's back to the way it was. I think the same holds true now as it did before Magic: **nobody thinks it can happen to them. Everybody went back to raging like rabbits.**

AIDS is just a figment of the imagination to people who are able to screw whoever they want, whenever they want. If you want it real bad, and it's right there waiting for you, you're going to do it and not give a second thought to AIDS. It's not right, but it's reality.

If you want it that bad, slickers aren't the first option. Guys might go out and buy condoms, but are they putting them on? I'd be the first to admit I don't always use the things. I've used them, but *sometimes the body doesn't listen to the mind,* and you don't reach for the condoms.

A lot of players tried to pawn off the AIDS "scare" by saying Magic must have had a gay relationship. People thought he must be bisexual, which nobody who knows him thinks he is.

But **IF MAGIC HAD A GAY RELATION-SHIP, THAT'S HIS BUSINESS.** If he was bisexual, that's his business. More power to Magic Johnson if he was gay or bisexual. Would that have stopped him from being one of the greatest players ever in this game? Of course not.

You don't look at what somebody's sex life is all about. He came out with HIV, and right away people were saying, "He must have been gay, that's the only way you can get HIV." But you can get HIV a lot of different ways. So who knows? You never know.

If it was me, and I had AIDS and I was homosexual or bisexual, I would come out and say, *"Yeah, I slept with guys. It's my fault. I should have used protection.* All I've got to say is I know I should have protected myself, but I did it anyway because of the hot, passionate sex that you want but can't get with a condom."

I would definitely come out and say that. I would have no shame in that, and people would respect me more because I had the courage to come forward and let the truth be known.

Magic's return to the NBA in 1996 was great for the league, and for people with AIDS or HIV. First he proved he could live a normal life, and then he proved he can still play basketball at the highest level in the world. When he made the announcement that he was coming back to play for the Lakers, there wasn't much discussion from players about whether it was safe for him to return, so maybe people have learned not to fear this virus so much.

When it came out back in 1992 that he wanted to get back into the league, Karl Malone was the most vocal opponent of his return. There were others—Mark Price was one—but Malone was the one everybody noticed. He was the most high profile, and he was the one who had the biggest problem with it. I don't think Karl Malone really gave Magic any credit. Magic was one of the main guys

Magic:
I don't care if the
guy I'm guarding
has HIV.

who made this league what it is today, and he deserved to be treated better.

This time, when Magic did return, Karl Malone said he respected the decision. To me, fighting Magic's return would be like saying you don't want anybody in the league who has herpes or gonorrhea. I know HIV and AIDS are on a different scale, **BUT I COULDN'T CARE LESS IF THE GUY I'M GUARDING HAS HIV.** If you know enough about the disease, you don't worry about it.

We played the Lakers in Magic's second game back, and I guarded him the whole game. It was the first time he'd faced real competition, because the Lakers played Golden State in his first game, and Golden State doesn't play any defense. I figured I'd welcome Magic back to the league the only way I know how: by bumping him and pushing him and treating him like any other player in the league. Like I told a reporter, I don't care if he's got HIV, measles, cancer, whatever. **I'm going to slam him anyway, and anybody who's got any balls will do the same.**

After that game, Magic and Michael Jordan had a big press conference, and they talked about how I muscled Magic and fought him every step of the way. Magic said he appreciated the competition, because he knew that was the only way he could get better. Then he said, "I think Dennis was trying to give this country a message. He hugged me, slammed me, beat on me, and nothing happened to him. So we don't need to worry about anybody else having anything happen to them." He drove it home when he said, "I think we educated a lot of people tonight."

I thought we did, too, but I never gave it a second thought. I hope we did educate some people—the people who might fear the disease for the wrong reasons. **If everyone had been better educated about HIV and AIDS, maybe Magic could have made his comeback sooner.** Or maybe he wouldn't have had to leave in the first place.

When I had the AIDS ribbon colored into my hair during the playoffs in '95, I became the first professional athlete to openly acknowledge the people who have AIDS. I was, without a doubt, the first one to make the statement so blatantly.

I did it because I wanted to do it. It wasn't thought out far in advance or anything like that. I do what I feel at the time, and at that time I felt like calling attention to people with AIDS. No other athlete had ever expressed his views that publicly, so I went to my hairdresser—who is gay—and told him to dye my hair green and dye the red AIDS ribbon into the back of my head. I figured, Let's put it on TV and recognize it. **Let all the AIDS victims know they're recognized and RESPECTED BY DENNIS RODMAN.**

I didn't hear anything from the NBA on that one. There's nothing they can say to me for doing something positive for people who are suffering. I didn't hear anything negative, and I didn't hear anything positive.

People would come up to me and say, "Hey, that's pretty cool the way you showed you care about people with AIDS." I also heard from a lot of people with AIDS after that. They just wrote to let me know they appreciated the gesture and were glad somebody in my position was out there thinking about them.

My teammates didn't say anything. Of course. They probably figured I was just off in my own universe again. **There is a lot of homophobia in sports,** and those barriers need to be broken down. Those people didn't do anything wrong to get this disease. They didn't try to get it. They didn't want to get it. It sounds stupid to have to say, but **people with AIDS are not bad people.**

AIDS has taken some of the enjoyment out of sex. If you're responsible, you've always got to worry about who has it. During the sixties, people fucked like rabbits; in the seventies, it was the same way. Now, in the eighties and nineties, if you're going to sleep with somebody, you've got to go in there with a Brillo pad and scrub a layer of skin off to make sure they don't have anything contagious.

I WORRY ABOUT AIDS. You have no choice but to worry about AIDS. It's out there. It changed my habits in many ways. I have to acknowledge that this is a disease that survives. It isn't going away anytime soon, so the only sensible thing is to take precautions and deal with it.

AIDS is a big issue in the NBA simply because sex is such a big issue in the NBA. **Players get into**

the league and they're interested in two things: *MONEY AND PUSSY.*

Management, coaches, the league—they know guys are going to go out and fuck; they know guys are going to go out and find any girl they can. It's not going to be hard either. They're going to find girls that are sexy as hell, good looking, sweet—all that. And they're not going to think for a second about the consequences.

I put it like this: I know *I've* done it. I've jumped in bed under a barrage of women, without even thinking about wearing a condom. I've gone from bed to bed. I haven't had a lot of girls, not like Wilt Chamberlain claimed to have, but I know what's it like to just go jump in the bed with a girl. I know what it's like to fuck without thinking about anything.

And now, even with Magic, I don't think habits in the NBA have changed. It's not like Magic sounded this big alarm that everybody heard. *UNPROTECTED SEX IS NOT UNCOMMON AT ALL.*

Everybody's aware of what AIDS is all about. The league informs and educates players. The only question is, do the players think it might happen to them? In the NBA I'd say the answer is no. I don't think most guys believe it can happen to them. It all goes back to fame and ego.

When you're in the NBA, you have everything. **IT'S NOT THE REAL WORLD.** You've got money, attention, women. Somebody picks up after you. You stay in all the best hotels. You're invincible. You can't die. You can't get AIDS, so you don't have to protect yourself. You just keep doing what you're doing.

nine

Man on Man

Painted Fingernails and the Status Quo

"**B**asketball is a man's sport." "Sports is a man's world."

Everybody has an image in their mind of what it means to be an athlete in our society.

I paint my *fingernails*. I color my hair. I sometimes wear *women's* clothes.

I want to challenge people's image of what an athlete is supposed to be. I like bringing out **THE FEMININE SIDE OF DENNIS RODMAN.** I like to shock people, to have them wonder where in the hell I'm coming from. To **hang out in a gay bar** or **put on a sequined halter top** makes me feel like a total person and not just a one-dimensional man.

I'm always looking for new ways to test myself, whether it's on the court or off. There are no rules, no boundaries—I'm trying to get deep into who I am. I'm trying to truly discover who I am. I don't think any of us really know who we are, and most people are afraid to let themselves go. They're afraid to take the chance, because **they might find out something about themselves they don't really want to know.**

Tomorrow I could bring a whole new, totally different dimension to myself. **IF I WANT TO WEAR A DRESS, I'LL WEAR A DRESS.** I'm up for just about anything; I'm still finding my way through the tunnels, looking for that light that gets me into the next version of the state fair.

Immediately, people are going to say: **He's gay.**

No, that's not what it means. I'm not gay. I would tell you if I was. If I go to a gay bar, that doesn't mean that I want another man to **put his tongue down my throat**—no. It means I want to be a whole individual. It means I'm comfortable dealing with different people in different situations. It means I'm willing to go out there in the world and **see how different people live** their lives. There's nothing wrong with that.

I grew up in a house of women—my mother and two sisters. **I thought when I was growing up that I was going to be gay.**

I thought that all along, because I had women around me and I wasn't accepted by girls. They thought I was unattractive, and I was so shy around them, it didn't really matter what they thought of me.

That's not to say I repressed my sexuality and now, all of a sudden, **I've decided I really want to be gay.** I didn't get money and a little bit of power and decide to let the real me loose.

Everything I do is about confidence. After years of struggling with my identity—who I was, who I was going to be—I've become totally confident about being who I am. I can go out to a salon and have my nails painted pink, and then go out and **play in the NBA, on national television, with pink nails.**

The opinion of other players doesn't make any difference to me. ***Most of them think*** I'M INSANE anyway, so nothing I do now is going to change anything. They look across at me with my painted fingernails and it gives me another psychological edge; now they're looking at me like **they really don't know what I'm going to do next.**

I have a pink Harley-Davidson, and I don't care what anybody thinks or says while I'm riding it. My pickup is pink and white. I'm confident enough that I couldn't care less if somebody thinks I'm gay. What I feel inside is this: I know who I am, and there's nothing you can say or think about me that's going to affect me.

It took me a while, but I have the same feeling of confidence and power in my personal life as I have on the basketball court. I took a lot of wrong turns and made a lot of mistakes, but I feel that I'm finally running my own show. Nobody's going to tell me it's not manly to drive a pink truck or wear pink nails. **I'll be the judge of my own manliness.**

There might be some players in the NBA who are gay. Would that shock people? Probably, but it shouldn't. There might be some players in the league who are bisexual. There are people in any profession who are gay and bisexual, so why should basketball players and athletes be any different? Statistically, it would be almost impossible for the entire sports world to exist without gay or bisexual people.

I'm not pointing the finger at any one guy, because I don't know about other players' personal lives. Also, I don't think it's something you stand around and point fingers about. You don't blame people for this, or ridicule them. If I was gay, I would stand up and say that I am. I would let everyone know that I am gay and existing in what is supposed to be a man's sport.

There is so much hypocrisy in sports, bro. Everyone is supposed to be tough and macho. Everyone's a man's man, tough and mean. But if you look closer, there are so many homosexual aspects of sports. It's all swept under the rug, though, because no one wants to admit the reality of things. Everybody says, "No way, that's just teamwork." Sure, we're all part of a team. Everything we do is all in the group, all in the family—

MAN on MAN.

Just look around. You'd be blind not to see it. Watch any basketball game. Watch any football game. What's the first thing guys do when they win a big game? They hug each other. What does a baseball manager do when he takes his pitcher out? He takes the ball and pats him on the ass. He could shake his hand or punch him on the shoulder, but he doesn't. He pats him directly on the ass. Isiah Thomas and Magic Johnson whispered into each other's ears and kissed each other on the cheek for years before games.

Man hugs man. Man pats man on ass. Man whispers in man's ear and kisses him on the cheek. This is classic homosexual or bisexual behavior. It's in the gay bible. You tell people this and they're like, "Oh, no it's not. It's just a man's thing."

And I say, **"YOU'RE DAMNED RIGHT. IT *IS* A MAN'S THING."**

I'm not saying you have to be gay to do these things, but you have to accept that it falls in the large confines of homosexual behavior. You just have to accept that. I do those things on the basketball court—hug a guy, pat a guy on the ass—and if you want to call me homosexual or bisexual because of that, that's fine. I accept that. Then I guess you can take the next step and say I want to sleep with a man.

After *Sports Illustrated* came out with the article in May of 1995—the one where I talked about fantasizing about being with another man—people have assumed I'm bisexual. I don't do much to discourage that, since it fits into my idea of keeping people guessing. I went to a T-shirt shop in West Hollywood during the off-season before I was traded to the Bulls, and I bought two shirts. On one it said, *I don't mind straight people as long as they act gay in public.* The other said, **I'm not gay but my boyfriend is.**

I wore the first one out to a club in Newport Beach the

next night, and this girl came up to me and said, "You're cool. You speak your mind, and that's what I like about you." Then she said, **"I'M BISEXUAL TOO— JUST LIKE YOU."**

I just laughed at her, and I didn't argue. Who knows? Maybe I am bisexual, but if I am it's in my mind only. I've never acted on it. Maybe I have this fixation that I want to be with another guy, but **is it so wrong to think that?** I don't believe so, especially when most people think about the same things—even if they don't act on their thoughts.

If you ask a man if he's ever thought about being with another guy, he'll probably say, "Oh, no. That's disgusting. I could never be with another guy."

Then you say, "Wait, have you ever thought about it?"

"No way. I can't believe you're even asking me. I've never thought about it."

To that I say, "Yeah, you have. If you didn't want to be with a guy, or **if you never thought about it, you wouldn't be so quick to say it's disgusting.** If you had never thought about it, you'd have to think about it before you gave me an answer."

I let people think what they want to think about me. I color my hair and paint my fingernails, and sometimes I wear women's clothing. I do it and watch people's reactions. Let them think what they want.

Gay men come up to me—and *on* to me—all the time. I'm very popular among gay men. I think I've done more to recognize them than any other professional athlete. When I put the AIDS ribbon on my head during the playoffs against the Lakers in 1995, I think that opened a lot of eyes. These people were finally seeing somebody openly recognize them. For the first time they saw someone openly show some support—with no embarrassment at all. It let them know there's someone in the sports world who understands and isn't going to pretend they don't exist.

I think **I'M NATURALLY DRAWN TO PEOPLE**

WHO ARE OUT OF THE MAINSTREAM. The people that society says aren't with the program are the people I'm most comfortable being around. No matter what city I've been in, I've always felt more at home when I go into a bad part of town and talk to some homeless people than when I'm sitting in some stuffy-ass restaurant with a bunch of people wearing ties.

The same holds true for gay people. They aren't fully accepted, and I don't think I'm fully accepted. We have something in common.

It came out in that same *Sports Illustrated* article that I go to gay bars. I do. I'm not afraid to do that, and I'm not afraid to say that. These people shouldn't be avoided or ignored. I think we can all learn something from them and from what they've been through.

Gay men always come up to me and say, "Thank you. Thank you for recognizing that we're not just a piece of dirt on the ground. Thank you for recognizing that **WE DO EXIST.**"

I've found these people want to be recognized as individuals and not just as a disease. They're not a traveling, walking disease—what some ignorant people consider a curse from God. They shouldn't be looked upon as people who shouldn't be here just because of one thing they do.

Whenever I'm staying in Orange County—which is whenever the basketball schedule allows—I go into Los Angeles and hang out in the gay community of West Hollywood. I love it there. I love going into that community. I love being in the gay atmosphere, because it gives me something I don't find anywhere else. It's free, it's open— **it's WIDE open.** That appeals to me. There's only one danger about being in the gay community: **THOSE PEOPLE HAVE NO FEAR OF ANYTHING.**

I think that comes from being through **SO MUCH HATRED** and **SO MUCH ABUSE.** When I went through all the racist bullshit in Oklahoma, it changed me. It changed the way I thought about people, and it made me tougher. It also made me look for something that could provide me with safe, solid ground. I found that with the Riches, and when I got some wealth and fame I got the safe feeling in—of all places—the bad parts of town.

Gay people are the same way. They create communities where it's safe for them, but they aren't afraid of anyone, and they aren't surprised by anything.

When I was young, I don't think I had a fear of being gay. I didn't really know what was going on, or what any of it meant. If I was going to be gay, it would have happened back then. I didn't run from it or keep it bottled up inside me.

I WAS ALREADY FUCKED UP, and having trouble deciding who I was going to be sexually was just another worry to throw on top of everything. I didn't really have to worry much about girls coming on to me when I was in my teenage years; I was already ***an*** **UGLY, BIGHEADED KLEPTO** *kind of guy.*

My curiosity about my sexuality has followed me to this point, this big stage. **Just because I can play a game and make a lot of money doesn't mean I suddenly have all the answers.** I'm open to everything, and I'm always asking questions. That's just part of who I am.

I can't say I haven't experimented with other men, but I guess it depends on what you mean by experimenting. I've kissed men, but it's like saying you kissed your little boy or your teenage son on the lips. I'm not afraid to go up to a good friend of mine and give him a hug and a kiss. There's nothing wrong with that, and I don't care who sees me do it. It's showing that I care about somebody. People think homosexuality is bad, evil. It's not bad at all, but people make it out to be just the worst thing in the world.

I've questioned my sexuality, but I've never found myself forced into a position where I have to decide whether to enter into a homosexual relationship. It's never been like that.

MENTALLY, I probably am *bisexual.*

I've thought about a lot of crazy things, and I've fantasized about a lot of crazy things. I don't know if I'll ever be physically bisexual. Someday I might be, but I haven't to this point. I haven't acted out on any of the things that have run through my mind.

I FANTASIZE ABOUT BEING WITH ANOTHER MAN, and I'm not afraid to admit it. You can't help but fantasize about it, if you ask me. If you're a free thinker and willing to let your mind explore like it wants, then you have to think about it. I believe it's natural for your body to go and explore anything it wants.

But you don't want to just jump into something because you've been thinking about it. It has to be something you can live with afterward.

When I go into a gay bar, I get approached by other men. Of course I do. They figure you're in there, so there's got to be a reason. But it's not like gay people come up to me and say, "If you feel the need to have sex with a guy, I hope I'm the one." It's not like that. If it ever happens that I do have a homosexual relationship, or encounter, it's not going to be a situation where I just decide I'm going to do it just to do it.

And here's something about the craziness of the sports world that I just don't understand: Whenever a sports figure does something that isn't manly, or if he does something in a way that is not considered manly, everybody gets all upset. It's like, "Oh, God—no way, not *him.*"

Why are athletes treated differently than people in everyday society? It seems that people feel threatened when an athlete does something that is not considered manly. It's like they've crossed over some imaginary line that nobody thinks should be crossed.

Entertainers and actors are not treated the same way. If an entertainer is gay, it's accepted. People accept that without a second thought. But somehow **it's always a scandal when an athlete comes out of the closet.**

There haven't been that many examples, and I think it's

because athletes are afraid of what might happen if they do come out. A baseball player named Glenn Burke had his career ruined because the Dodgers apparently found out he was gay. The team couldn't handle it, they couldn't deal with it. Teams can deal when a guy has a drug problem or an alcohol problem, but not when they find out someone's doing something they don't like in the privacy of their own bedroom. **IT DOESN'T MAKE SENSE.**

Maybe when an athlete comes out, people start to wonder: Is the world of sports turning into a gay world? I guess athletes are supposed to be completely different from any other walk of life. If a guy who works in your office is gay, it's no big deal. He's just gay. But if a guy who plays basketball or baseball or football comes out and says he's gay, everybody looks at him funny. Nobody can believe it. That doesn't make any sense to me. We're held to a different standard.

People look up to us, and why? I think I have an answer: More than anything else, people play sports and listen to music when they're looking to escape their lives. Or they watch sports and read about sports and talk about sports. So with so many people interested in sports, there's no way it can be accepted if somebody within that community comes out and says he's gay. People trip on that.

This isn't something I can talk to other players about. I can't open up and say, "Have you ever thought about being gay?" There's not a player out there who would say, "Yeah, you know I have. **I wish I was gay. I wish I could be.**" No way a player would ever tell you that, even if it was true.

I'm not trying to encourage kids to be gay, but it shouldn't keep them from being in athletics if they are. You can't say I'm less of a man because I've given some thought to being with another man. I'm not trying to steer kids into saying being gay is cool. **YOU GO WITH YOUR HEART,** your feelings, and what you desire. Like anything,

Don't let what other people think decide who you are.

WhEN I go on road trips, I sometimes laugh to myself when I think about everybody's luggage coming off the plane and down the conveyor belt to the baggage claim. Everybody's luggage is there, with all their fancy clothes, and then there's mine, carrying my jeans, T-shirts—and some women's clothes.

There might be **A SEQUINED HALTER TOP** in there. There might be some **WOMEN'S LEGGINGS** in there. There might be some **TIGHT LEATHER SHORTS** in there. You never know what might be in there.

I'm guessing here, but I imagine I'm the only guy in the NBA who packs these kinds of clothes on the road, then wears them out to bars and clubs. And I know I'm the only one who would come out and admit it.

I've got no problem admitting it. I can be the only guy in the world doing it and it wouldn't stop me. I don't think many people think about who's cross-dressing after the game when they look out there and see all these guys running up and down the court, playing this man's game. **Nobody I've ever played with knows I go out and dress in women's clothes.** They know I dress in wild, crazy clothes, but when they're looking at it, they don't know if it's women's clothes or just gay clothes.

Sometimes, I admit, it's hard to tell. **When I made a presentation at the MTV Music Awards, I was cross-dressing.** I wore a woman's top and my fingernails were painted. It wasn't obvious that I was wearing women's clothes, but if you looked closely you would have known.

The first time I painted my nails was on Halloween of 1994. I had them painted orange and black, and people looked at it as more of a stunt than anything. **Just RODMAN**

With Christopher Walken at the MTV Music Awards.

One of us was cross-dressing.

being RODMAN again.

Now I don't even think twice about my nails; I get them done all the time. About once a week I'll go into a salon and have them done. It's just something different, and I like to look down and see the different colors.

I don't think painting my fingernails is a big deal. It's not like I'm sitting home by myself, trying on lingerie. That's not my style. I don't do lingerie. I think cross-dressing, the way I do it, is more accepted than people think. Look at all the clothes now that are made for both men and women. You go into a store and sometimes it's hard to tell whether you're in the men's or the women's section.

It wasn't that long ago that everyone freaked out when they saw a man wearing an earring.

I grew up around women, and as a kid I would sometimes dress up as a girl. You play house, you play doctor—everybody does that, but some people like it more than others. You play by dressing up and acting like a woman. I think a lot of kids have done that. I used to go through the whole routine—**dress up, wear makeup, act like a girl.**

When I cross-dress now, it's just another way I can show all the sides of Dennis Rodman. I'm giving you the whole package. I'm becoming the all-purpose person. I'm like the running back that can break one to the outside and also go over the middle to catch a pass.

I'll do this wherever I feel comfortable doing it. It doesn't matter where. If I feel like dressing up, I pick my time and place. I've done it in New York, Los Angeles, Chicago, Detroit, and Dallas. I go into straight bars, gay bars, it doesn't matter. **I'm not afraid of doing it anywhere.**

In New York I go to the Channel Club or the Tunnel. Those are two of the places I feel comfortable wearing my clothes. I'll go out with friends I know from different cities, but never players. Other than Jack Haley I'm not hanging out with any players on the road.

Cross-dressing is like everything else in my life: I don't really think about it, I **JUST DO IT.** I don't remember the first time I decided to do it as an adult; there isn't one time that really sticks out. It was more of a gradual thing, where it progressed from earrings and fingernails to halter tops and tight leather shorts. I've done it since my early days in the NBA, but I've started to do it more often since I made the decision—back in the cab of that pickup, in that empty parking lot—to live my life the way I want to live it.

I haven't worn a dress, yet, but I did buy one to wear on the Howard Stern show one time. It ended up that I didn't get out of bed in time to get it on. I had to rush out of the hotel and get to the interview, which was at seven in the morning.

I LIKE TO WEAR TIGHT STUFF, AND I LIKE SEQUINS. I usually wear shirts and shorts and jewelry. I wear different earrings when I wear a halter top. **I wear *women's leggings* under my clothes,** but no lingerie. I haven't gotten to the point of wearing high heels either. I just wear my normal leather construction boots, the ones I wear all the time anyway. **You'd be surprised the kind of clothes you can get in my size.** I buy all the stuff myself. Nobody does it for me. I go into women's clothing stores; I don't have a problem with that. I'm not going to call somebody and have everything custom-made, because that's not my style. Besides, that's sort of like hiding it. I could have someone come out to my house and measure me and all that, but half the fun is seeing the looks on people's faces when I go into the stores and try things on.

The salespeople love it. They can't believe there's **a big, macho basketball player coming in and buying women's clothes—**and buying them for himself.

There's another thing I found out right away: girls love it. They *love* it. Guys say, **"I wouldn't wear it, but it looks good on you,"** but girls go crazy over it. They love to see a guy who's not afraid of his manhood. They love it when a guy has all the confidence in the world, enough to paint his fingernails pink or ride a pink Harley-Davidson. They love a guy who can wear a sequined halter top and be very comfortable.

Everything depends on how I feel. I'm not more likely to cross-dress after we've won, or after we've lost. I don't choose my spots like that. I just go by what I'm feeling at the time, and what kinds of emotions I want to express. **IF YOU WANT TO DRESS, YOU DRESS.**

It's total freedom. Totally. It's the freedom to be who the fuck you want to be, and nobody else matters. It's just another side of me, one that most people are afraid to show. There are all these sides I'm discovering, and I don't know how many are still out there, waiting to be discovered.

ten

Madonna

An Old-Fashioned Tale of Romance

The first night I was with Madonna, we ended up in a gay nightclub in Miami. I was sitting at a table, having a drink, staring out at Madonna and her girlfriends on the dance floor. They were dancing, and then some. Madonna was dancing around, hugging these girls, holding these girls and kissing them.

It was playful and fun, and I was in the middle of the whole thing, watching and wondering what the hell this crazy life had done to me this time. Little did I know THIS WAS JUST THE BEGINNING of a wild six months.

Madonna first came into my life in 1994, when she was going to all the Knicks games at Madison Square Garden. She was there along with all those other stars—Woody Allen, Spike Lee, Billy Crystal. She liked John Starks at the time, but I never paid much attention to her love life, to tell you the truth.

Then, during the '94 All-Star Game, she was on television saying she really wanted to meet Dennis Rodman. She said something like, **"I think DENNIS RODMAN is COOL AS SHIT.** I think he's his own person. I think he's for real, and I want to meet him."

I wasn't even in that All-Star Game. I averaged 18.3 rebounds a game that season—led the league, of course— but I didn't make the All-Star team.

From there it was about three months of this public- -relations person talking to that public-relations person, trying to set up a meeting with Madonna and me. The way I looked at it, if the woman wanted to meet me, *let's just meet and get it over with.* Let's not deal with a hundred different people just so we can sit down and talk. Finally, in April, one of her people called and asked me to come to Miami because Madonna was going to interview me for *Vibe*, the hip-hop magazine. They told me the magazine had assigned her to do an interview of me, and it was supposed to be the cover story—with photos and the interview—for the June 1994 issue.

To be honest, I thought **IT WAS ALL A BUNCH OF BULLSHIT.** I didn't think it would ever happen. What did this woman want with me? The PR people were jockeying around forever, trying to figure out how we could get together. The whole time they were telling me she was doing her research on me for this interview. I didn't believe a word of that, to tell you the truth.

But when it came time to go, I figured, what the hell? Another adventure.

Because this was during the season, the plan was for me to fly from San Antonio to Miami after practice on an off day, do the interview and the photo shoot, and get back to San Antonio in time to be at the game that night.

I went with my friend Bryne Rich down to Miami to meet her and stay at her house. I wasn't going to let Bryne miss out on an opportunity like that. When we got there, we went to the door and a girl, Madonna's manager, answered. We went in and Madonna came down the stairs to meet us.

I looked at it as just like meeting anybody else. Just

another person. I wasn't all starstruck about this thing. I said, **"I'm DENNIS,"** and she said, **"I'm MADONNA,"** and we both said, "Great." This was Madonna and all that, but I was like, "Cool—Madonna. No big deal." This wasn't like my dream or anything, and I couldn't imagine it was hers either.

I didn't like her work at all. **I didn't like her music.** I told her that too. I thought she was a brilliant entertainer, but her music wasn't my style. She changed with the album called *Bedtime Stories*. It was pretty cool, but a lot of people didn't accept it.

After we went through the introductions at her house, she did the interview. She sat there and took notes and everything. She had questions ready, all written down. After we did some of the interview, they started doing the photo shoot and ***we were just all over each other.*** From the first photo we were covering each other. I didn't care if it was Madonna or not, to me

it was just another girl and we were on each other. They ended the photo shoot before we got too carried away. We ended up going out to the gay bar—that was an experience. She wasn't mobbed there, because the people

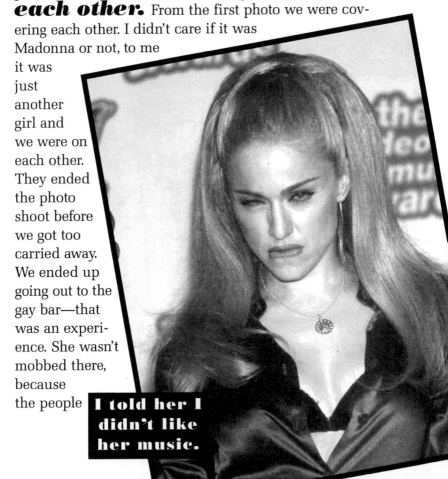

I told her I didn't like her music.

knew her and were used to her. She liked to go to familiar places in Miami, places where it wouldn't be a huge deal for people to see her.

Eventually we went back to her house. I got in the house and headed for the spare bedroom. I was all set to just go in there and crash, but Bryne was already asleep in there.

Before I could ask where I should go, Madonna looked at me all sexy and said, **"YOU'RE STAYING WITH ME, IN MY ROOM."** There was no doubt. She wasn't going to let me go in that other room, whether Bryne was in there or not. Then she shut the door and told her manager, "He'll be with me."

So I laid my head where all the other mongrels had. First thing you know—boom!—we're messing around. We sort of picked up where we left off during the photo shoot, except this time there was nobody watching.

After we kissed for a while, she stopped and looked at me.

"Are you going to **eat my pussy** first?" she asked me.

I said, "Oh, is that the way it is?"

"That's the way it is," she said.

"Believe me, I won't do that, darling."

She said, "You aren't going to just eat me out? That's what I like to get me ready to go."

I said, "No, can't do that."

She said, "I like someone to eat me out and get me loose."

I didn't do it. I think she was a little surprised that I said no to her, but I did: **I said NO to Madonna.** A lot of guys don't believe I could turn her down, but I did.

It didn't end there, though. She got over it. She started stroking my shaft and getting into it, and before long I was inside her and we were fucking. I would say I was making love to her, but you don't make love to a woman the first night you meet her.

We went at it for a while, me with Madonna, right on her bed. I could tell she liked it, because she was into it. **She wasn't an *acrobat* or anything, but the *sex was good*.** There's some passion there, and she isn't afraid to let it out. At that time, I figured that would be the end of it, that I was just another in a long line of fucks.

Bryne and I flew home the next morning, and almost **as soon as I walked in the door MADONNA CALLED.** Then she called again that night, and again. She called and she called and she called. She called nonstop, and she sent me faxes all the time.

This was pretty wild. I didn't know how to take this. What I had thought was an excuse to get together with Dennis Rodman became a real relationship. She wanted to be romantic. I'd thought she was looking for sex, but she was looking for someone to take care of her. It wasn't about being nasty or kinky. She was looking for the right man for her, and I was the prime chosen one.

There was one thing she brought up all the time: She wanted to have a child. She talked about that from the beginning. She called me the "prime physical specimen" for her child. **She wouldn't let me wear a condom—NEVER.** She wanted to get pregnant really bad. She would send me faxes that said, "I really want to be with you, I miss you." Regular stuff like that. But then there were others that said things like, "I want every drop of your come inside me. I won't let it go because I want to have your baby."

Madonna talked all the time about having a baby. All the time, bro. She wanted it so bad, so bad it was hard to believe. I think she wanted every bit of Dennis Rodman— **MARRIAGE, kids, everything.** She felt she had finally found the one she could be on the same level with, and she wasn't going to let it get away.

She was the one who put forth all the effort in the relationship. When she first decided to get us together, I think she just wanted to find out what kind of person I was and then fuck me. At first I think that was her intention. She didn't really want a serious relationship, as far as I could tell. It was just going to be a fling and that was it.

As it turned out, the *Vibe* magazine story was real, but it never appeared in the magazine. I found out later they didn't like the way it turned out, so they scrapped it. They were going to make it the cover story, but the interview didn't turn out the way they expected.

Our relationship had better luck than that article. We got to know each other and we found out we had a lot in common. Our philosophies on life were pretty much the same. We thought a lot alike, and we both have the same knowledge about how stupid life is on this marble we live on. **We are two people who do whatever we want in life and get away with it.** We see through the shit,

Tita and Daddy Longlegs

both of us.

Athletes and entertainers aren't all that different. We came at things from the same angle. She knows she's not going to be a sex goddess her whole life, and I know I'm not going to be a superstar athlete much longer either. You can't hold on forever, and both of us understood that. We weren't living in a fantasy world, making ourselves believe we'd have everything we have now for the rest of our lives. We both wanted to experience as much as we could while we still had it going for us, though.

And we both understood **the BULLSHIT PEOPLE feed you when you're famous.** We knew who our friends were and who the people were who were in it for themselves. We both had a lot of experience with that.

She started getting into me because she saw that I was real. She saw I was totally unlike most of the other people she dated or knew. She saw something in me. I couldn't figure it out. What was I doing with her? It was like I was in a different world.

One thing I couldn't do, though: **I couldn't bring myself to call her MADONNA.** I just couldn't see myself saying, "Hey, Madonna." It just didn't sound right, bro. Too weird. She came up with a name for me; she called me "Daddy Longlegs." I called her "Tita." I don't know where that

name came from, but I just liked it and decided to call her that. It just came to me, and I figured *What the hell? It sounds cool.*

One reason she was attracted to me is because she likes basketball players. She even talked about buying a team there for a while. She was with Brian Shaw when he played for the Miami Heat. She could say **she made Brian Shaw. She gave him an identity.** I didn't need that. She told me Brian Shaw went around flaunting it, that he loved it. I told her, **I ain't Brian Shaw.**

"I don't give a fuck who you are," I said. "If I'm with you, it's because I want to be with you, not because you're Madonna and you can help me get noticed."

Basketball players to Madonna are like ballet dancers or any kind of dancer. She feels basketball players and dancers are both graceful and elegant. Very sleek. She enjoys that part of it. Athletes are a real turn-on for her because she appreciates anybody who can move with such fluid motions.

MADONNA'S A CONNOISSEUR OF BODIES. She studies them and watches them closely. When you've been around the world as much as Madonna has, you've probably seen more things than anybody. You should be a connoisseur of something, and for her it's the human body.

She looks at a basketball player and she wants to know how he can do the things he does. It really interests her, and she sets out to find out whether it's something she wants in her life every day. She can have anybody in the world—every man thinks she's the ultimate fuck—so she can choose who she wants.

I guess she decided she wanted me.

Anybody who dates Madonna is **going to get attention.** If some guy nobody knows dates Madonna, everybody is going to know him before long. When I was with Madonna, the attention was incredible. It was unlike anything I'd ever been around, and some people probably thought I was with her just to get that attention.

The truth was, there was a lot more to it. The attention that came with being with Madonna was the worst part of being with Madonna. She was great, but I could do without the other stuff. If you want to know why I'm not still with her, you can start right there.

I still didn't understand how serious she was until the day she showed up in Utah. Utah was huge, bro. We were playing in the first round of the playoffs against the Jazz, and Madonna flew in from Los Angeles—she has a house there, too—to watch us play the third game of the series.

I couldn't believe that she would fly out there to **watch me play basketball in Bumfuck, Utah.** Who wants to go to Utah, especially someone like Madonna? She had come to our last regular-season game, but that was against the Clippers in Los Angeles, and she was already in Los Angeles. This was a different story altogether.

She told me she was coming, but I didn't believe her. I said, "Yeah, right—I'll see you when you get there." I was at the hotel the day of the third game, just hanging in the room, and she called and said, "I'm going to send a limo to pick you up."

This was some SERIOUS SHIT. If all you're interested in is sex, you don't fly to Utah to be with the person. There was more to her interest in me than just sex, and I should have acknowledged that to her right away. I should have thanked her for coming, and I should have told her I understood how much of a hassle it is for her to go anywhere, but I didn't pick up on that like I should have. I figured she just had some free time and decided to come pay me a visit. I think I was still a little blown away that she was interested in me, and my mind didn't let me believe it was anything more than a fling.

The third game of that series was on May 3, 1994. We

lost the best-of-five series in four games and I got the blame—of course—because **I WAS A BIG DIS-TRACTION AGAIN.** I was a distraction because of Madonna and I was a distraction because I didn't play in the third game.

I was out because I was fined $10,000 and suspended for—as the league put it—hip-checking John Stockton. I did it. I admit it, but you have to remember the point I made earlier: **John Stockton is the cheapest cheap-shot artist in the league.** He gives more cheap shots than anybody I know. They also got me for hitting Karl Malone—I still don't think I touched him—and coming down on Tom Chambers from behind with my elbow, sort of a tomahawk job.

All I can say is, it was a physical series.

So I got blamed for losing that series, never mind that **David Robinson didn't come to play—again.** I got blamed because I got suspended for a game and because Madonna showed up for Game 3 in Utah.

I didn't stay with the team in Salt Lake City. Here was my choice: stay in the Marriott with a bunch of guys, fight the autograph hounds, sit in my room and watch television, or stay in the mountains in a three-bedroom condo with Madonna. Which would you choose? She rented a place in a resort above Salt Lake City. The condo was gated off, with a limo waiting outside the door. For me it wasn't a hard choice.

That limo was like my shuttle bus for those few days. I'd sleep up in the mountains, then take the limo down to practice or the game, then take the limo back up the hill afterward. I could have gotten used to that lifestyle very easily.

Madonna's fame is based on sex, and she is very passionate, but she wasn't the kind who wanted to do it three or four times a day. She just had to **get her one good one in,** hoping it was **the one to make her PREGNANT.** A lot of people would say to me, "Having a baby with Madonna? Look at

Should I stay with the team, or with Madonna?
Hmmm.

it this way: This time you get the child support." That's how people were thinking; nobody thought it was anything more than a couple of celebrities messing around.

Other than what I did on the court, I didn't want to have anything to do with the team during that stay in Utah. I didn't even tell the coaches or team management where I was. Jack Haley was my only real friend on that team, so I told him where I was staying and what I was doing. I gave him the phone number and told him he could give it out, **"IN CASE OF EMERGENCY ONLY."**

This was all a big deal, of course—a distraction. Same story as always with me. But the deal is, who were the ones who ate it up? ***The team ate it up, and John Lucas ate it up.***

There was Madonna, sitting at the game, and everybody was just flipping out. I was like, Damn, what you expect me to do? I'm going out with her. What do you want me to do? Other guys have their girlfriends there, don't they? Or their wives? Just because my girlfriend happened to be the most famous female performer in the world, I couldn't bring her to the games?

In Game 3, the game I was suspended, the team played terribly. We lost 105–72. It was embarrassing, just awful. David Robinson had 16 points and 11 rebounds, but he was not a factor. You want to know how bad that game was? Jack got big minutes in that game—and he had a big game. **David did nothing in that series.**

I watched that game up in the mountains with Madonna. We sat around that condo and watched it. I was suspended, so I didn't go. ***If they weren't going to let me play, I had better things to do.***

We never should have lost that series. We won the first game at home, then lost three in a row. Our season ended right there. The last game was close—95–90—and I had 20 rebounds, but that team didn't have the heart to go any further. We blew them out in the first game and then lost three straight.

After the final game I walked into the locker room, grabbed my stuff and got into the waiting limousine with Madonna. I didn't say anything to anybody. I left before Lucas could give his end-of-the-season speech. I didn't shake hands with anybody or say good-bye. My season was over. **There was nothing they could tell me that I didn't already know.** I threw on my warmups and left in my uniform. My next stop was Los Angeles, where Madonna and I hung out at her house.

That was in early May, and we spent a lot of time together after that. I saw her in New York and L.A. We spent a week and a half in Atlanta, at the Ritz-Carlton, while she was recording an album.

Everyone in the Spurs organization—and some players—criticized me for taking away from the team because Madonna was there to watch me play. They didn't like it that I wasn't staying with the team, but you want to know the strangest thing about that whole Madonna deal? Everybody wanted it to happen. Everybody was so taken by her being with me. They were like little kids.

It was like that from the beginning. The first time everybody saw Madonna was at the last regular-season game of that season, against the Clippers in Los Angeles. That was the game David Robinson scored 71 points and nailed down the scoring title. Among the team, the big story wasn't David, it was Madonna in the stands, watching me.

I think it was a joke that everybody involved with the Spurs thought I was a big distraction because of Madonna. I was the one trying to play it down. **I was the one trying to keep my off-court stuff off the court.** I wasn't the one who dragged her into the locker room after that game. John Lucas was. I wasn't the one standing outside the locker room taking pictures with her. The other players were. I didn't want her in the locker room. I didn't think it was fair to make her parade through the locker room just because she was going out with me.

John Lucas came up to her after that Clipper game and

193

grabbed her—*grabbed* her—and walked all the way back into the locker room with her. This was the head coach. And who was sitting there saying, "We got to get Madonna. We've got to get Madonna here for this game"? It was the Spurs organization; they were the ones saying that.

Nobody brings that up. Nobody tries to say the Spurs organization—or John Lucas—was a big distraction to the team because of the way they acted when Madonna showed up. No—I was the big distraction.

I wanted to see her, but I didn't want her to come to the games. I knew people were going to make a big-ass deal out of it. They wanted her to come to the game because they knew it was going to be a big-ass crowd. Let's have a crowd. Let's have everybody come out and see Madonna.

But she wanted to come to the games, and that's her right. If she wants to come and watch a basketball game because she's going out with a guy on the team, nobody should make her feel uncomfortable. **JUST LET THE WOMAN BE, BRO.**

After that game against the Clippers everybody was all jacked up. It was like a big party. Everybody wanted pictures with Madonna. Even Jack Haley's family got into the act, wanting pictures. Everybody wanted something from her and from me.

There was so much confused emotion going through my head at that time. There were so many mixed messages being sent my way. They wanted me to be with Madonna, but when I was with Madonna, I was a big distraction. It didn't make sense.

There was nothing in it for John Lucas, so I don't understand why he got so excited. He ate it up, more than anybody. It was just Madonna. That's the way it was: Madonna's at the game. Look at Madonna.

Other players were like that too. **They made it a CIRCUS.** The NBA made it a circus, the Spurs made it a circus, my teammates made it a circus. There's Madonna, sitting in the front row, watching Dennis Rodman. **CAN YOU BELIEVE THAT?**

194

At that point in her life Madonna was ready to settle down. She was really cool to be around—mellow, low-key, caring. She has this public image of being hard and tough, but underneath that she's a sensitive person. She likes to be held and comforted.

I wasn't ready to settle down, though. She wanted me to calm down a little and be happier just hanging with her and living a slower lifestyle.

She used to say, "I've been through that stage. I've been wild and crazy." **She wanted me to get through my wild stage, too,** but I couldn't just drop everything. I was still having fun, still looking for new challenges. I wanted to go out on my boat, hang with my friends, but she couldn't do that. If she did, everyone would have gone ballistic. **She was always looking for places where she could BE A PERSON and NOT MADONNA,** and that was hard for her. She couldn't just come down to Dallas and hang out with me and my friends. They'd be too freaked out, and it would end up being a bad situation.

I don't have to be hidden behind closed doors. The way I look at it, if people get used to seeing something, pretty soon it's a regular thing. Before long, seeing me out at a club isn't a big deal. I tried to get her to go out, but I think she's pretty much afraid of going out. In her position, there's a little fear about what people might do to her. **YOU NEVER KNOW WHEN SOME CRAZY PERSON IS GOING TO START STALKING YOU** when you're that high-profile, like that Hoskins guy who said if he couldn't have her he'd slice her throat from ear to ear—the guy her bodyguard shot. She couldn't even go out to dinner that easily; there's always the chance people would mob her, swallow her up, and not let her move.

In a way, it's sad. She's such a prisoner of her fame. She can't do the kinds of things normal people do. Almost

195

everywhere she goes is a big fucking scene. People notice me and bother me for autographs and everything, but I'm not going to let that keep me from doing the things I want to do. If I want to go out, I'll go out. I want to be as normal as I can be. Madonna can't really do that. There are just a few places she can go to be normal.

She's a great lady. If you watch her on TV or in her videos, you get the perception of her as a real hard person who says "Fuck" for twenty minutes on David Letterman. In person, ***she's nothing like that.*** I don't remember her swearing to excess when we were out together. She always handled herself elegantly.

We never had any problems. It was one of the easiest relationships I'd ever been in. The sex was great—not the greatest, but good enough—but there was more to it than that. We understood each other so well, it was almost scary.

But as sweet as she was, whenever I was with her I always knew I was around a woman who had power and knew how to wield it. She is a big-time businesswoman, and she knows exactly what she wants. Just look at the way she got me to come to Miami: she got hooked up with *Vibe* magazine, then used that to get me down there. She wanted to meet me, so she made it happen.

She can have anybody she wants. She's got all the money in the world. She's a powerful woman. That's what appealed to me about her. **There was nothing else in it for her.** There was nothing I had that she wanted. There were no strings; it was all just liking the person and enjoying being with them. I didn't have to wonder whether the roof was going to cave in and she was going to start wanting my money. Hell, **MY MONEY WAS POCKET CHANGE FOR HER.**

And the sex was very entertaining, which helped. It was entertaining but it wasn't something that needs to be exploited. It wasn't wild, crazy, and kinky. It wasn't like that at all; it was just very entertaining.

Everybody thinks she would have the greatest, wildest

sex in the world, and every guy wants to sleep with Madonna. I got to where I didn't think of her that way. We were comfortable together, and the sex was perfectly natural and satisfying. **SHE WASN'T AN ACROBAT, BUT SHE WASN'T A DEAD FISH EITHER.**

I HAVE TO COME CLEAN ON ONE THING: The whole time I was with Madonna, I had a girlfriend named Kim. She was living with me in San Antonio, but the relationship was messed up because I thought she was lying about who she was. She also kept saying she had all this money. It turned out she was feeding me a bunch of lies and that made it easier for me to see Madonna with a clear conscience.

Kim knew I was seeing Madonna, and that caused some problems. She knew our relationship was dead. She saw all those faxes and letters from Madonna. She knew I was talking to Madonna all the time. We broke up, and I started seeing Madonna more.

After we broke up, I took Kim to Las Vegas. I wanted to go to Las Vegas, and I didn't want go by myself so I took Kim. The first night we're there, Madonna's assistant comes up to me at the craps tables and says, *"There's someone who wants to see you upstairs."* She didn't normally travel with an entourage, but she brought it along this time.

I'm thinking, *Oh, God.* And MADONNA WAS RIGHT THERE. She tracked me down in Las Vegas. I'm there with Kim, and Madonna found out and followed me. She was not only there, but she was **IN THE ROOM *RIGHT NEXT DOOR.*** She found out what room I was in and got herself hooked up with the one next to it.

Madonna knew I loved Las Vegas, and when she found out I'd left San Antonio, she went to Las Vegas. I guess anybody could do that with me, because I'm pretty predictable that way. When I go party, I go to Las Vegas. When I go to Las Vegas, I stay at the Mirage. Madonna figured that out, then found out what room I was in and got the one next door. I told you—she's one woman who knows what she wants and knows how to get it.

So after Madonna's assistant got me, I left the table—by myself—and went to see Madonna. We were in the stairwell, and she was saying, **"YOU LOVE ME. YOU WANT TO BE WITH ME. LEAVE WITH ME RIGHT NOW AND FORGET YOUR GIRL-FRIEND."** So what did I do? I think obviously I did the right thing by going and getting my shit and leaving with Madonna. We got on a plane and went back to her house in Los Angeles. Kim got home okay, but there wasn't much left of our relationship after that.

Madonna has done a lot for gay people, and I've tried to do the same. She expresses it in her music, and I expressed it by getting the AIDS ribbon colored into my hair during the playoff series against the Lakers my last year in San Antonio.

Madonna and I are similar in some ways. Madonna sometimes acts bisexual—whether or not she is—and I think of myself as being bisexual in my mind only. Madonna is not addicted to sex. She doesn't go out to a club, pick out a girl and say, "I want to sleep with her tonight." I think she expresses it in other ways. If she wants to be caressed by another woman, then she gets caressed by another woman. But she doesn't go out looking for a woman to do kinky things with.

She always asked me, *"Do you like seeing me together with my girlfriends?"*

I'd tell her right out: **"NO."** I think she liked that more than anything. All the guys she's with are usually into that. That was a big turn-on for them. They wanted to be with her when she was with her girlfriends.

I wasn't interested in that, and I didn't have the chance

if I was interested. She never hung out with her girlfriends when I was with her. After that first night at the gay club I didn't see her with another girl the whole six months we were together. It's not because I controlled her—no way. She just wanted to be with me, and me alone, when we were together. **WE HAD A GOOD THING.**

Jack Haley used to go out with us sometimes, and afterward he'd always tell me, "You guys are in love, bro."

She had to pick and choose the places we could go out in public. We tried to go to places where she was used to being seen: gay clubs, small bars near her house. I always wanted to go somewhere else, somewhere bigger, with more people.

I think Madonna started to realize I wasn't going to settle down. I told her that too. That was one thing about this relationship—we were totally honest with each other. I told her that **HER HOUSE IN LOS ANGELES SUCKED.** It just didn't feel like a home; it felt like a cold, empty place, not a place you could feel comfortable just hanging out in. Her house in Miami was great, though—huge, right on the water, just perfect. She told me, "If you get traded to Miami, you can stay here. Just move into my house."

I told her, "I can't stay here. This isn't my house."

"If we're together, this is your house," she said.

That's the way she treated me. She was very generous, very open. I think she'd been hurt in the past and didn't want to go through that again, so when she found somebody she was comfortable with she really wanted it to work. I didn't look at her as Madonna, and I think she appreciated that. I looked at her as a person who is successful but vulnerable just like everybody else.

She didn't push me, other than showing me she cared about me, but it was clear the opportunity was there for marriage if I had been thinking that way.

Sometimes I don't know why I didn't follow through and go after her more seriously. I liked her because she had a brain, and she had made her name and her money on her own—just like I did.

In the end it didn't work because **_I didn't want to be known as Madonna's playboy, HER BOY TOY._** I didn't want people thinking of me as Madonna's quack-quack duck in the bathtub. I didn't need to be thought of as something she could just play with whenever she was ready.

I know she didn't think of me that way, but a lot of people looked at it like I was. **That bothered me, I admit it.** Normally I don't give a shit what other people think about me, but this time I just didn't think I could deal with it.

Maybe I gave in to appearances on that, but I think **BEING MR. MADONNA WOULD HAVE BEEN A TOUGH THING TO OVERCOME.** I didn't want what I had created on my own to be mixed up with what being with her would have created. **It was a very confusing time,** I admit that, but I just couldn't see myself getting seriously involved with her knowing everything that would have come with it.

I think I've created an image where everybody recognizes Dennis Rodman for Dennis Rodman, and not for Dennis Rodman with Madonna. If I was with her, everything would have always been linked with her.

Besides, I don't know if I could have made the commitment she wanted. I don't know if I could have been there as much as she would have needed me. She was looking for a guy who's going to be her right-hand man, her soulmate. She wanted someone who could be there to protect her.

I still have feelings for her. I still think back to things she said, the way she felt about certain people, and **_sometimes I wish I would have done more to make it work._**

She lives in a world where all anyone thinks about her is that she's wild, sexy, and crazy. But there's another side to her, a softer side she keeps to herself. I got to see that side.

WE HAD SO MUCH IN COMMON. Everything she's doing, everything I'm doing—we're a totally perfect match for each other. I thought we were, and she knew we were.

I would tell people, "I think she's in love with me."

They'd say, "You've got to be kidding."

"No, I'm not kidding."

She hadn't been in love with somebody that much since she was married to Sean Penn. I came along at just the right time, and I think she thought she'd found Mr. Right.

We don't talk anymore. I think it hurts her to talk to me now. I'm not going to force the issue. I've tried and it didn't work out the right way. But now I don't force the issue at all. *IF SHE WANTS TO TALK, SHE CAN CALL ME.* She knows where I am, she knows how to reach me. I think more than anything, she won't talk to me because it would really hurt her.

She knows she has these feelings for me, or at least she did, and now everything is broken. It shattered in her face, even though I didn't want it to. I just want to have my own identity and not have to live my life in the shadows of her fame. I think that overcame any feelings I had for her.

She used to always say, "You have to understand, people are going to say things when you have a relationship with me. They're going to say you're doing it just to improve your status."

"I've got no problem with people saying that," I said. "But I don't want you doing certain things to help me."

That's what I told her. I didn't want anybody thinking I was piggybacking on her. I thought about it a lot, and I knew that a lot of the shit that I would have gotten, I would have gotten because of Madonna. I don't want that. *I'm not one of those leeching sons of bitches.* I want to earn everything I get.

She didn't become angry with me, just sad. I put some effort into it, but only when it was on my terms. I never took it too seriously because after we had fucked and been seen together,

I couldn't figure out what she wanted with a guy like me. I can't compete with any of these other guys she's had.

I still think of myself as this guy who had to claw his way up from a job as a janitor to get anything in life. So to be making a decision on how serious to get with Madonna was more than I could handle.

There was more to it than just a game. I wasn't just trying for a good score. It wasn't a game. So I made love to Madonna. That wasn't what I was after. I was on the Howard Stern show and he kept talking about it as a good score, and I think that probably hurts her to be thought of that way.

When I was with Madonna, the attention was unbelievable. Everywhere we went there was a collection of photographers. Everywhere we went. I was like, "No way." Everyone wanted that relationship so bad. When they first learned about it, you could almost hear them say: "All right." This was something. This was the biggest thing the NBA could ever hope for, to have **THE TWO CRAZIEST PEOPLE IN THE WORLD BE TOGETHER.**

When we first got together, I pictured her house being covered with photographers, but they didn't hang out around her house. It wasn't that bad. It was just whenever we went out, they were there. I don't know how they find those things out, but they just appeared like magic whenever we got to a restaurant or a club. When they find out where the huge stars are, people are there.

I didn't look at it like, "Wow, I'm with a famous person, *THE MOST FAMOUS WOMAN IN THE WORLD,* the diva of sex." I never looked at that. She never came up to me as the Goddess of Love. It was more like coming upon somebody who was **JUST SO UNIQUE.** It's very rare that you can find someone to go out with that is truly unique.

When we were together, it was a lot of fun. It was great. It was two very independent people wanting to make a cosmopolitan type of relationship. We wanted to have independence together—at least I did—along with everything else.

Since then, I've found that a lot of girls want to be with me because they know I was with Madonna. They think that's cool. They think since I've had the so-called Goddess of Sex, they want to see if they can compete.

Whenever I hear that, I just laugh. I can't understand why people care about that kind of shit. Madonna was the ultimate celebrity girlfriend, I guess, but I never thought of her like that. It never dawned on me. It wasn't "Madonna, Madonna, Madonna, I dream and lust over her." She was a cool chick once I got to know her. That was about it. The whole power thing wasn't a part of it.

Everyone says she dumped me, but it was the other way around. Everyone assumes because it's Madonna, that she dumped me. **She dumped me because I wouldn't see her so many times.** If you want to call that her dumping me, go ahead.

Madonna and I had one last chance to get back together during the summer of 1995. We were together for three days in Los Angeles, after everything had fallen apart and we had gone our separate ways. I didn't think we'd ever spend any time together again, but we wanted to see if we could make something out of it. **There was still a spark there, and we needed to see if it would catch fire.**

I came out to L.A. for a week and stayed at the Hotel Nikko. She came to see me three straight days and we talked about it and talked about it. There were paparazzi everywhere—just everywhere, bro. Jack Haley came to visit me and I was carrying his baby boy—he was six months old—out of the hotel. All the paparazzi and the reporters were yelling, **"IS THAT MADONNA'S BABY?"**

It was wild. The child was white, blond, and blue eyed—good call on their part. **LOOKED JUST LIKE ME.**

When she came to talk to me, it had been almost a year since we'd been together. She came and we just talked. It was nothing sexual, no talk of having babies or anything. We just talked, trying to see if we could work this thing out, and I guess we found out we couldn't.

After that week in Los Angeles, when nothing came of it, everybody said, "Oh, she really kicked him out this time." I was there, and that's not what happened.

Nobody understands that. She's Madonna, so everyone automatically thinks she gave me the boot.

I heard her during an interview ask, kind of playfully, "Do you think I should marry him?" It sounded to me like I didn't have any say in it. I was sitting back saying, **"No, I don't think you should marry him without him saying something about it."**

I didn't want "Madonna the Rock Star." I've had her, done her, it was great. What I wanted was the cool person I hung out with and shared some great times with. In the end we found out there was too much in the way for that to happen.

I don't think it'll be dead between us until she gets married. Then it might be dead. But there were so many strong feelings there; it could happen where we get back together. If I wanted Madonna right now, if I went on an all-out assault—call in the brigade—to get her back, she would respond. If I cried out and said I long for Madonna today, something would happen. Believe me, bro. That's what happened the last time.

The whole time I was with her, I couldn't get one thought out of my mind: **I HAD NO BUSINESS IN THIS SITUATION.** I wasn't starstruck, but at the same time I didn't know how something like this had happened to me. Of all the unlikely things that have happened to me—getting out of Dallas, making the NBA, becoming a star—this was the hardest to understand. This was Madonna, a romance with everybody watching.

I'd tell her, "I shouldn't even be here. You want somebody else, you don't want me. **YOU CAN DO BET-TER THAN ME."** I always told her that, and she would say, "I think you're good enough. You're good in bed, and if I find someone who's good in bed, I feel comfortable with them. You're it."

I've been trying for a long time to stay normal, to be treated like a regular person. Being with her, that was impossible. I couldn't be normal. I would have had to fight all those old battles all over again.

At one point she came up with the idea that **she was going to drop everything and move to San Antonio.** She was going to come and live with me in my house. She saw that as the solution to all the problems, the one way of cutting through everything and making it work.

"I was going to make it easy for you," she said. "I was going to bring my life to you, but you just wouldn't take it."

She would go on and on about that. She would cry for me, and I knew she was serious. The problem was, I just couldn't respond to it. It just wasn't there, bro. I just didn't feel it. **I JUST COULDN'T BE MADONNA'S BOY.** In the end, when I had to make that decision, I couldn't give up everything I had to chase that dream.

eleven

Death Wish

Living Fast and Hard

I **LOST $35,000 IN LESS THAN A WEEK** at the Mirage in Las Vegas during August of 1993. I stood in that casino and let them have my money. The more, the better.

It seemed everyone in Detroit was looking for me. They were joking about **putting my face on a milk carton.** Training camp was coming up—my last training camp as a Piston—and the team had no idea where I was. I didn't want them to know either. That was why they didn't know.

Part of the Rodman legend is that I set out to lose that money, that I walked into the casino with $35,000 in my pocket and decided to see how fast I could turn it over to the house.

That might make for a better story, but it isn't all the way true.

I started out wanting to win. I always gamble to win. But when I started losing, I had a thought: *Lose it all.* Just put it all on the table and lose it. **Give it to some-**

body else and let them deal with the problems that come with it. At the time that's all money meant to me: problems. As I stood in that casino watching my money being swept off the tables, I didn't care if I ever had a buck to my name again.

At the roulette wheel I put my money on red and rooted for black. At the craps tables I chose numbers and hoped I was wrong. Just like so many other times in my life, I wanted to go back to where I was before I had all this. I wanted to go back to a time when I didn't have $35 to lose, much less $35,000. I wanted that feeling again, that feeling of hunger and survival. I wanted all that to kick in, and the only way I knew to do it was to throw all that fucking money on the table and lose it all. ***I needed to be desperate.***

Money complicates things, so the obvious cure was to lose the money. I think I need life to be hard. I sit in front of my locker before games listening to Pearl Jam, and **I PUT MY MIND IN THE WORST POSSIBLE PLACES.** I put myself in a hospital with dying children, and from my locker I can feel all the pain and suffering that they feel. The music goes through me and puts me there. The music is about pain and suffering, and how you can't run away from it. I need that to break loose and remind myself that it wasn't always so easy. I put my mind on the streets, with people who are homeless and hungry, and I tell myself I'm out there playing for them. I have to think of the worst to make sure I don't get lazy or start taking things for granted.

That's what I was going through at the casino. I wanted to feel that pain of having nothing. I wanted to be that rookie again, **the guy who hyperventilated while signing a contract and ran around in practice like his shorts were on fire.** That was the guy people loved. **THAT WAS THE GUY I LOVED.**

I wanted to be normal again, free of all the shit that comes with people knowing who you are. Las Vegas is the place I go to feel normal, to be among people. What better place than Vegas? You stand there with everybody else, putting your money next to theirs, hoping for the same thing.

This was a bad time for me. My marriage to Annie had **broken up,** Chuck Daly was **gone,** the team was **going to hell** and I was **CONFUSED.** I didn't know what I wanted, but I knew I didn't want what I had. I needed to get back to the times when nobody knew who I was, and when **PEOPLE WOULD SLOW DOWN IN THEIR CARS TO YELL AT ME AND CALL ME NAMES.**

I was real popular in Detroit, but when it came time to talk contract I was at the bottom of the list. This is when I realized there was no commitment, no loyalty, no nothing. This is when I started to lose some of the thrill the game provided, because I was realizing the business side of it sucked.

My short-term answer was to lose the money and try to trick my mind into believing I had to fight and claw again to make it back. I wanted the pain.

The preseason before my last year with the Pistons was one of my lowest points. I felt betrayed by the Pistons, and I wasn't able to see my daughter. I didn't hide how I felt, either. I sat in my house in Bloomfield Hills and didn't come out. *I used to lock myself in my house and not answer the door;* I didn't want people to know where I was. I would go out after midnight to work out at Gold's Gym or buy some food.

I've done that since I've been in Chicago too. I go out and work out at midnight or one A.M. I like having the place to myself, and I like the feeling of doing something like that while everybody else is lying in bed.

When I was going through all that crap in Detroit, I changed my phone number a bunch of times. Each time I did it, I told the phone company not to give me the number. I figured if I didn't know it, nobody could call me and bother me.

I get depressed when I'm frustrated, caged in, but the more I train my mind to feel that depression, the stronger it makes me. Instead of avoiding it and trying to feel better, I give in to it and let my body feel it. When I do that, it takes me back and gets my mind right. **When I hit bottom, I can attack the problem and get to where I want to be.**

It's no accident that I had a great season my last year in Detroit. With the team falling apart and my life all messed up, I still led the league in rebounding with an average of 18.2 a game.

I don't trust what this life has given me. I don't trust the money or the attention or the people telling me they love me. I don't trust it because I know it's going to be gone. It's temporary, and once your career is over, everybody forgets. There's somebody else out there for them to idolize, and if you're standing there, old and washed up, asking these people, "Hey, what about me?" then you're sad and pathetic. I see former players coming back all the time, and they're searching for what they used to have. I'll never be like that. **Once I'm out of the NBA, they'll never see me again.** I'll move on and make something else of my life.

I know this attention isn't always going to be there. I know it's only there for a short time, and the people who give me the attention aren't in it for me—they're in it for themselves. *It's all about what they can get out of me.* You're crazy if you buy into it; if you don't know why it's there in the first place, you won't understand when it's gone.

If I die young, everybody's going to say they saw it coming. They're going to say I had a death wish, that I was crying out for help and nobody heard me.

Or, more likely, they're going to say I was on drugs.

I know what the average guy in Minnesota or Utah thinks of me. I know he sits down in front of the television with his beer and says, **"That guy with the green hair's either CRAZY or ON DRUGS."**

I know that's what people think, and I say let them. I can't change anybody's mind, so they can think what they want.

The truth is, I've never even smoked a joint. I've never tried cocaine or acid or any other drug. I don't need drugs to keep myself going. I don't need drugs for energy or fun or to escape whatever's going through my mind.

Drugs are in sports, but not as much as they used to be. They used to be more in the open, but now they're behind the curtain. ***Wherever there's money, there's drugs, so to say drugs don't exist in the NBA would be stupid.*** But guys know the score now. They know they can throw their whole career away if they want to hand it over to drugs. Most guys now are educated enough to stay away from it.

When I first got into the league, Rick Mahorn called me aside and said, "Come with me and hang with me. I'm going to show you the ropes." That whole unit was pretty much like that. John Salley and I were rookies at the same time, and the older guys told us about life on the court and off. They told us what we could accomplish if we kept our minds straight and removed the distractions from our lives.

The year I was drafted by the Pistons, the team's top draft pick was William Bedford, a seven-foot center out of Memphis State. He could have been a great player; he had an incredible amount of talent and a great body for the game.

When William showed up, it turned out to be my turn to try to help somebody. I wish it would have had better results.

I think we all saw right away that Bedford didn't want it as much as he should have, but we didn't realize how big his problems were.

I can remember walking into his room on the road and

knowing right away there was something wrong. It was dark and cold. The air conditioner would be blowing in the middle of winter. William would be sitting in there, just staring. Before long we all realized this guy—a guy with all this talent—was putting all his money up his damned nose.

I used to try to make sure he was on time for the bus on the road or practice at home, but he didn't seem to care. We all thought we could get him straightened out, but he was in too deep. He failed a few drug tests and eventually got *flushed out of the league.*

If I ever needed any more motivation to keep away from drugs, William Bedford gave it to me. He kissed all his talent away. In four years with the Pistons he averaged 3.5 points per game. When I think of how good he could have been, and how much better our team could have been if he hadn't been taken down by drugs, it almost makes me want to cry. That guy had everything and ended up with nothing.

Whenever people think I'm on drugs, I have one answer: Ten years in the league. That should be all I need to say, because **THE GUYS WITH THE DRUG PROBLEMS DON'T LAST.** William Bedford didn't last. Chris Washburn was another one: he was a top pick of the Golden State Warriors the same year I came out, 1986. He left North Carolina State after his sophomore year and never amounted to anything in the NBA. He failed drug tests and ended up throwing away all his talent too.

Look at Roy Tarpley. He lasted longer than most, because he got so many chances. But he had a $23 million contract, and he kissed it off. He failed test after test, and finally he failed one too many and the league policy called for him to be finished forever.

When I first came into the league, I could have gone toward drugs. Anyone who plays has the opportunity. I still do. I'll go into a club somewhere and someone will shake my hand and try to pass on a blotter of acid. The first time it happened, I was looking at this little piece of paper not knowing what it was. Then somebody told me it was acid. These people—never an NBA player—just want to be able to say *they dropped acid with* **DENNIS RODMAN,** or they smoked marijuana or did cocaine with me. They say it anyway, even though they haven't, so I guess I can't win. I don't need drugs, though; I get enough of a rush from going out there and playing basketball.

I'LL GO ON NATIONAL TELEVISION LIVE, RIGHT NOW, AND TAKE A DRUG TEST. I'll take one every day for the next month.

In sports, drugs have gone behind the curtain more than they were before. Everyone is aware of what can happen if you get caught: you lose your whole career. With everything available to an athlete he has to sit down and ask himself the question: **What's going to keep me going over the long haul, drugs or the game?** What's going to give me the security and money to last my whole life?

It's not just athletes who have to ask themselves these questions, it's everybody. You have to ask yourself if you're going to rely on your own gifts to take you where you want to go, or are you going to take a chance on living through this lie?

Sure, drugs can put you over the top all right—**over the top so far, you'll fall back down and land in a six-foot hole.**

I THINK ABOUT DEATH A LOT. I'm not afraid to die. I'm going to keep living the way I do—hard, fast—and I don't really care if anybody out there thinks I have a death wish. That's what I hear a lot: Dennis Rodman has a death wish.

I DO HAVE A DEATH WISH. It's there. That doesn't mean I'm living with an eye on death. It doesn't mean I'm secretly crying out for someone to stop me before I kill myself.

My death wish is there because I'm not afraid of death. If I crash my Ferrari and die, it was just meant to be. If I die on my motorcycle, it was meant to be. I just don't want people feeling sorry for me, saying they should have stopped me before I went too far. No. When I die, I die.

The only part of death that scares me is the pain. Why die with pain? I don't want that kind of pain. I'd rather just leave this world before the pain hits. I probably won't live to be an old man. **I'm already old for where I came from.** From the projects? I'm already old.

After the police found me in The Palace parking lot, the Pistons made me see a psychiatrist. The guy told me there was nothing wrong with me. "You're not crazy," he said. "You're not crazy at all."

Before the 1994–95 season, the Spurs put me on paid leave when I was holding out because they went back on their promise to give me a new contract. They made me see a psychiatrist, and that guy said the same thing as the first guy.

"You're not crazy," he said. "They're just not used to dealing with somebody like you, and they don't know how to handle it."

I think people throw out the idea that I'm crazy or on drugs just because they're trying to find an easy way to explain the way I am. Instead of trying to deal with it, they just **put me in a box that says CRAZY or DRUGS** and they have an answer for everything. They can say I take my shoes off on the sideline because I'm crazy, and not because of the problems I have with my feet. They can say I drive my Ferrari fast or gamble or ride in my speedboat because I have a secret wish to die.

Some of the stories about me are so far gone, it's not even funny. People think I'm capable of anything, so they'll believe whatever somebody says about me. I've had people tell me they read where I take my uniform off at halftime of games and put my street clothes on. Then, somehow, I change back into my uniform in time to warm up for the third quarter. I don't know where that started, but people take it as the truth because they're willing to believe anything about me.

The truth is, I take my shoes off at halftime, and sometimes I'll take my uniform top off and throw on a T-shirt.

It's all my way of feeling comfortable, letting my body breathe and feel free. But if people want to think I'm in there putting on my pants and lacing up my boots during halftime, I guess there's nothing I can do to stop them.

I'm more interested in taking my clothes off than putting more on. Another reason people think I'm crazy is that **I want to play my last game in the NBA in the nude.** I said that to a reporter, and it became this huge thing. I know I won't be able to play the whole game naked, but I might be able to work something out.

After my last game, here's what I plan to do: I'll walk off the court and take off one piece of clothing with every step. First it'll be my shirt, which I'll autograph and hand to some kid in the stands. Then I'll toss my shoes into the stands, then my socks, then my shorts, then my jockstrap. Then I'll be at about midcourt, and I'll walk the rest of the way into the locker room nude. Nobody's ever done that before, and it can be **my parting shot to the NBA.**

If I die young, everybody will say, "It was drugs. It's got to be drugs." That will be the first thing out of everyone's mouth. Then they'll say, "He was suicidal. He was suicidal from the beginning, just look at the way he played and what he did off the court."

After my rookie year I went back to Dallas to see some friends from the neighborhood. One guy is a big-time drug dealer, and he wanted to take me out to this club where a lot of dealers and drug people hang out. We walked into this place, and we weren't two steps inside the front door when **SOMEBODY AT THE BAR PULLED OUT A GUN AND TOOK A SHOT AT US.** My friend was out of there in a flash, and I followed after I realized what the hell was going on. We raced to the car and got away before they could chase us.

I was sitting in that car with my head down, thinking,

I'm an NBA player. What the fuck am I doing here?

That story never made it into the newspapers, probably because it was before anybody knew who the hell I was. But can you imagine the headlines if that happened now? DENNIS RODMAN SHOT AT WHILE LEAVING BAR WITH DRUG DEALER—that would be all over the place. And everybody would say the same thing: They knew it all along.

Everything's based on image—no matter what the real story is—and I've found out that **corporate America can be scared away** when it comes to somebody who's a little different. I was all set to sign a big endorsement contract with Robitussin during my last year with the Spurs, but they backed away when they read Mike Silver's story in *Sports Illustrated* in May of 1995.

In the article I talked about being with another man, and about my thoughts on killing myself, and I think that scared Robitussin off. They said the image in that article didn't fit the image they have in mind for their company. I said fine, that means *YOUR COMPANY'S IMAGE DOESN'T FIT MY IMAGE,* either.

I see they ended up with Shaquille O'Neal's mom. I guess that's more in line with their image.

When I was sitting in the parking lot of The Palace that April night in 1993, with the gun beside me, I had to ask myself whether I really could go ahead and kill myself that easily. Once I knew I could do it, I tried to come up with another way of dealing with my problems. It was like I hit bottom and then started to climb out.

One thing I was fighting was *whether I should pull the trigger* and have a quick death or go on the way I was and make it a slow death. The way I was living back then, I was on the road to a slow death.

Now I'm happy with who I am and the life I'm living. I won't live the life other people want to see me live. I know what people think, and what people say, but it passes right through me. I've survived through so much shit that I don't think there's anyone who can tell me how I should live. I've been given a lot of second chances during this wild life, and this time I'm getting to live on my terms.

I'll know when my life is complete when there's nothing left for me to accomplish, when there are no goals or dreams. When I get older and that happens, I'll probably go somewhere out of the way—the woods or the mountains—and spend some quality, private time with myself. I'll go over everything I've done in my life and spend some time thinking about it. THEN I'LL TAKE OUT A GUN AND SHOOT MYSELF IN THE HEAD. That's how it will end, right there.

twelve

The Big Distraction

Taking the Blame in San Antonio

The San Antonio Spurs went into the playoffs in 1995 with the wrong idea. Most of the guys on that team, and the coach, thought we could roll to the NBA Finals because we led the league with 62 wins during the regular season.

But once you get to the playoffs, the regular season doesn't matter. Nobody cares how many games you won. You can't play the playoffs like you play the regular season. You need an extra gear. You need to be able to take everything—family, friends, hangers-on—and remove them from the equation. You need to be able to **play physical, kick-ass basketball, and play it every night.**

That team never found the extra gear. That team didn't have the heart to do what the Pistons teams did when I was in Detroit.

Insubordination?!

SHIT, my feet are like gnarled

The team got a lesson in playoff basketball, and I got a lesson—another lesson—on what it's like to be sold out and left hanging, alone, to **take the blame for a whole team's failures.**

It started to fall apart in the Western Conference Semifinals against the Lakers. In Game 3 of the series, which we lost, I came out of the game in the second half and took my shoes off on the sideline. This was no different than most other games. I didn't see a place for me to sit, so I lay down next to the press table that ran behind the baseline. So there I was, shoes off, towel over my head, kicking back watching the game.

Then, during a time-out, I didn't get up. I didn't join the huddle. I sat where I was, watching. The television cameras caught me the whole time, just like they always do, so the whole world saw me sitting there, back against the press table, with my shoes off.

Bob Hill didn't like this. Gregg Popovich didn't like this.

I didn't play anymore in that game. Nothing was said to me; I guess it was just supposed to be understood that I wasn't going back in. After we lost that game, we still led the series, two games to one, and the Spurs decided to suspend me for Game 4. They said the suspension was for "insubordination." Then, after we won that game, they decided I wasn't going to start Game 5.

I understand that it didn't look good for me to be lying over there when the rest of the team was in the huddle. I understand that. But I also think they made way too much out of it. They let themselves be so distracted by me that the team lost its focus. They couldn't just let me be myself for a while and deal with it another time. They had to make a big deal out of it, right there, because they wanted to make sure I knew who was boss.

THEY TREATED ME LIKE A CHILD AGAIN. I got out of line so they had to sit on me.

The players wanted **old tree branches.** to take a stand against me. Management wanted to take a stand against me. The whole organization wanted to send a message to me.

Some of the players—**DOC RIVERS** is one guy I remember—**SAID I WAS BEING IMMATURE** and doing things to hurt the team. That's when I first realized I wasn't going to be back the next year. Players started deciding I wasn't worth the trouble, that *the team would be better off without me.*

The suspension was Popovich's decision, but I believe he had the approval of the coaches and players. They weren't going to say anything he didn't want to hear.

If another player had done what I did, I wouldn't have given a rat's ass. So what if a guy didn't go into the huddle. Like I said before, there are so many guys in the huddle who aren't paying attention—what's the difference? I wasn't in the game, I wasn't going back into the game right away, so why did it matter? It's all appearances and image, and I wasn't representing the Spurs the way they wanted to be represented.

None of the players stood up for me. I lost a lot of respect for the guys on that team when that happened. They left me out there, hanging, just to save themselves. They played it safe. They knew it wasn't good for the team to make me sit out, and they knew what I did wasn't the worst thing in the world, but they **didn't have the guts to stand up and say something.**

This is the playoffs, and they were more worried about sitting on me than winning the games. I had a hard time understanding that.

It all goes back to the same thing in this game: money. Whenever there's money on the line, everybody's hush-hush. ***If a guy has a contract on the line*** that year, or the next year, he's not going to go against the general manager in a situation like that. **He's going to sit there with his mouth shut, trying to be Mr. Nice Guy,** because he doesn't want to say something the boss doesn't want to hear. ***If you sell your SOUL, that's what happens.***

I'm not sure, but I think these were the same players who were coming up to me at the beginning of the Lakers series, talking about what we'd done in Detroit and what we needed to do to win it all. They would come up to me before games and talk about championship basketball, asking me for tips on how to play certain players, what to look for from the referees, how to turn the intensity up.

In the end, though, everyone looks out for themselves. A player who's near the end of his career isn't going to say anything, because he knows he could be gone if the general manager doesn't like something he says. Who's going to stand up and say something? A guy who's up for a new contract isn't going to say anything. A guy who might be looking for a new contract from that general manager a year or two down the road isn't going to say anything. Sometimes it doesn't take much to piss off management, and **nobody's going to put themselves on the line for someone as unpopular as me.**

I DIDN'T LIKE THE COACHING IN THE **PLAYOFFS.** Simple as that.

Bob Hill coached the conference semifinals and the finals like we were playing Minnesota in the middle of December. He was going with a nine- and ten-man rotation. You don't do that in the playoffs. You don't sit me out for long stretches when I'm the team's best rebounder, best defensive player, and the only guy standing there with two championship rings. It's ridiculous. You play six or seven guys in the playoffs and make sure your stars are out there for forty minutes a game. That's the only way you can win.

With Phil Jackson, Michael Jordan can go 3 for 18 and still play more than forty minutes. You can't give up on a guy because he starts out badly.

It was real easy for them to take a stand against me after we'd won the first two games of the series at home. Everyone thought this was some bold move on their part, but I would have liked to see what they would have done if we hadn't been up two games to one when they decided to suspend me.

After we lost Game 3, we won two of the next three to advance to the Western Conference Finals against the Rockets. **THEY WON IN LOS ANGELES WITHOUT ME.** I admit that. I sat and they won. It worked out perfectly for the Spurs: they got another chance to show they were "taming" Dennis Rodman, and the team won the series. Perfect.

The television cameras were on me the whole series in Los Angeles, and again against the Rockets. I was like this sideshow to the game, and they didn't want to miss anything—on the court or off. **It seemed like they had a camera just for me the whole postseason.**

I think that attention made the Spurs do what they did. I've been taking off my shoes on the bench for years; that wasn't anything new to anybody on that team. I did that in Detroit, and it was never an issue. I do it because I want to let them breathe, and I want to feel free when I'm not in the game. My feet get sore when I'm playing, and taking my shoes off when I'm not in the game helps me feel more comfortable when I'm in the game. **It's not like I'm taking my shoes off to shove them in somebody's face.**

There's a reason for it.

But once everybody in the country saw me without my shoes on, the Spurs—and probably the NBA—decided something had to be done. They couldn't be seen as having lost control of one of their players. There's an image to protect—the image of the NBA Man.

After we beat the Lakers, we had three days to wait before playing the first game of the Western Conference Finals against the Rockets. The Rockets went seven games to beat the Phoenix Suns, and the last game of that series was May 20, two days after we finished off the Lakers.

I wanted to go to Las Vegas during that time off, so I did. I went with my friend Dwight Manley and Mike Silver, a reporter from *Sports Illustrated.* **THIS, OF COURSE, DROVE EVERYONE ON THE SPURS CRAZY.** They didn't know where I was, and they were worried that I'd just bailed out on the team.

Jack Haley called me in Las Vegas and told me everyone was panicking. He told me I had to get back to San

Antonio that Saturday night, May 20, to attend a team dinner with everybody and their wives. Then Bob Hill called and told me I better be there—or else. So that was my choice: stay in Vegas and have fun or go back to San Antonio and sit around with everybody and their wives.

What I really wanted to do was fly from Las Vegas to Phoenix for the seventh game of the Rockets-Suns series. I wanted to just walk in and sit courtside to blow everybody's mind. They'd be thinking, **WHAT'S WITH THIS GUY? HE'S EVERYWHERE.** I thought that would have been really cool, to show up there to see who we were going to play.

That's the aura I want to throw out there: a guy who's everywhere. When somebody tells me my hair is going to fall out because it's been dyed so many times, I tell them when it all falls out I'm going to get two eyeballs tattooed onto the back of my head. Eyes in the back of my head—how perfect is that? I'm going to do it too—**SO EVERYBODY KNOWS I'M ALWAYS WATCHING.**

Anyway, I went back for the team party. I listened to Jack Haley and Bob Hill and I decided to come back. Jack was the only guy on that team I could talk to, and I think the Spurs used him to get to me. Everybody around the league—and all the fans—thought that **Jack was like MY BABY-SITTER.** That's how he's always described, as either my baby-sitter or my translator.

I let that go. If people want to believe that, fine. Jack knows he doesn't have to wake me up for every practice. He knows I care about the game and work hard to keep myself in shape to play. It got to the point in San Antonio where people didn't think I could get to a game or practice without Jack leading me by the hand. Jack and I are friends, and sometimes he advises me on what's best for me, but sometimes Jack talks too much like a coach. I tell him that, too, all the time.

I let Jack have all that. I don't argue with anybody about it. If it helps Jack, that's fine. What I didn't like was the way the Spurs used Jack. They used Jack to talk to me, then they went behind Jack's back and started talking shit about him. They said, "Jack Haley ain't shit. He's only here because of Dennis." That isn't right. Treat the man right. They told him he was the middleman and the go-between—and **they kissed his ass** the whole time they were trying to get him to play that role—***THEN THEY BACKSTABBED HIM.*** They listened to him and took his advice, then they talked bad about him.

Typical.

After the second game of the Western Conference Finals against Houston—after we fell behind two games to none with two losses at home—Avery Johnson stood up in the locker room, in front of the whole team and most of the team's management, and said:

"We can't wait for David Robinson to take us, because he ain't going to be there for us."

David Robinson was there, sitting right in the middle of everyone. When Avery was finished, David was still sitting there. He sat there and took it.

We lost that series in six games, and the Rockets went on to sweep the Orlando Magic in four games to win the title. I guess you could say, based on that, we were the second-best team in the NBA. That's not good enough, though, because I think **WE COULD HAVE—AND SHOULD HAVE—BEATEN THE ROCKETS.**

I got blamed for losing that series, of course. Everyone says I sold out the Spurs, that I didn't play, that **I was a major distraction.** It's gotten to the point where the incidents in those two play-off series—Lakers and Rockets—have become the defining point in my career.

I say there are two sides to that story.

Where was David in the Houston series? *He got eaten alive* by Hakeem Olajuwon that whole series. They asked me to guard

Olajuwon, and I refused. Bob Hill came up to me and asked me if I would take Hakeem in the first half, and I said no. I would have taken him in the second half, but not the first. Any coach will tell you don't put your best defensive player on the other team's best offensive player in the first half. You put it all on the line in the second half. That's how it worked with Chuck Daly in Detroit, and I know that's how Phil Jackson feels in Chicago.

What you try to do is contain the guy in the first half and make sure your best defensive player doesn't get into foul trouble early. **You've got to be physical with Hakeem,** and I'm no good if I've got three or four fouls in the first half. Then every time I touch somebody, it's a foul. Against Los Angeles in the semifinals I couldn't touch Elden Campbell without being called for a foul, and Elden Campbell doesn't get the breaks from the refs like Hakeem does.

So if you want me to guard him in the second half, fine. David got into foul trouble against Hakeem just by falling down. David asked me for help, and I told him right to his fucking face, "I am not going down there." I was not going to help him. He didn't say anything to me, because there was nothing he could say. Before those games, *HE LOOKED SO FUCKING SCARED IN THE LOCKER ROOM, HE COULDN'T STOP SHAKING.*

They asked me to double-team Olajuwon, and I refused. The way the defense was drawn up, there was no way I was going to be able to get back down inside when my man was out at the top of the key or way out on the baseline. The defense didn't make sense, and I told Bob Hill this. He just looked at me and said, "This is the defense we're going to run."

In practice every day Coach Hill would say, "David, you think you can play Olajuwon straight up?" David would just shrug and say, "You all can come down and help if you want." Never once did he say he could take him by himself. This guy was **the MVP of the league,** and they were paying him **$8 MILLION A YEAR.** He needed to step up and at least say he could do it by himself. He was supposed to be the one leading this team.

They were paying David all this money, and never one time did he stand up and say, "Don't worry about it. I've got him."

Those guys screwed me over for two years, and then they came to me and asked me to bail their asses out. That's what it came down to. I did what I had to do. I got them to the Western Conference Finals. I got them there, and we should have gone further.

In that series against Houston I played. **I PLAYED HARD.** I'll say that to the day I die: I played. People say I played as an individual, that I wanted all the glory. If you believe that, you haven't been paying attention; you don't know me or my career.

I helped that team, but they didn't listen to me until it was too late. We lost the first two games—at home, even— because the defense we were running was ridiculous. David was getting killed inside, and Robert Horry was killing us from the outside.

Do you want to know who changed the defense for the next two games, after we got to Houston? I did. I saw what we were doing wrong, and I set out to change it. I finally got Bob Hill to see it my way, and it worked. David played Hakeem straight up. Hakeem got what he was going to get anyway, but we stopped everybody else. That's the whole key to stopping them: Give Hakeem what he wants and clamp down on everybody else. **It's not that hard to figure out.**

We won those two games in Houston to tie the series at two games each. In the fourth game we blew them out, 103–81. They scored only 81 points against us, because we were playing defense the right way. We were heading back to San Antonio for Game 5, tied at two games. Even though we started out the series so badly, we were going home having to win two out of three, with two of them—Game 5 and Game 7—at home. It looked like we finally had our act together.

So what happens when we go back home? Hill decided to go back to the defense we were running in the first two games. It was unbelievable. We went back to double-teaming way outside and getting our ass kicked inside. Then we switched up and collapsed inside so they'd throw it out to the shooter—Horry—and he killed us on three-pointers. We made Horry a star in that series.

The Rockets beat us two straight and went to the Finals. **I was so *PISSED OFF,* I couldn't believe it.** After the Spurs traded me, Bob Hill described my season by saying, "Dennis did not ride with us on the team bus to the first practice of the year, and he wasn't with us after the last game of the playoffs. You take it from there."

I wasn't with them after the last game because I didn't need to be with them. We lost Game 6 in Houston to end our season, and I went off on my own. I didn't need to sit there with them and have everybody slap each other on the back and pretend we did all we could. We had a good season, but **we didn't do what we could have done.** We let it slip away, and I didn't feel like pretending it was okay.

I talked to Phil Jackson, and he told me the same thing: David would have to play Hakeem straight up in that situation. With the way Horry and Kenny Smith can shoot the ball outside, there was no other way: David would have to play him man-to-man, straight up, no help.

You can blame me—I don't really give a shit—but ***where was Sean Elliott?*** Did he ever stop Clyde Drexler? Was there one time when Sean stopped him? I say no. Clyde lit Sean up for 30 a night—every night. I don't blame Sean, because there was one guy on that team who could shut down Clyde, and that was me.

One more time I ask the question: ***Where was***

David? When he couldn't handle something, they asked me to help him. I'm not going to help him. Fuck that. Who's out there helping Sean Elliott? Nobody. So they want me to shut down Hakeem, and who's going to stop Clyde? Nobody.

IF YOU'RE THE MVP OF THE LEAGUE, YOU'VE GOT TO STAND UP AND DO THE JOB.
The bottom line is, I didn't like the coaching. If they want me to take all the blame, fine. I'm man enough to take the blame. I did some things I shouldn't have done in the playoffs. I admit that. I'm big enough to admit that. But why can't they admit what they did? Where was David Robinson? Where was Sean Elliott? The only guy on that team who stood up like a man and played in the series against Houston was Avery Johnson.

Bob Hill wasn't ready for the pressure of that kind of series. He didn't know how to handle it. If I'm the coach, I'm going to let David Robinson get his ass kicked. That's just what John Lucas used to do. It goes back to what we used to do in Detroit. We knew we couldn't stop Michael Jordan, so we let him get his 40 points and set out to stop everybody else. What the Spurs did against Houston was try to stop Olajuwon and everybody else. We were trying to do everything, and instead we did nothing. We left ourselves open inside and outside.

Hakeem was INCREDIBLE. By taking that team to its second straight championship, he moved up into that level of Michael Jordan, Magic Johnson, and Larry Bird. He was doing whatever he wanted with Robinson. He'd start on the baseline and hit that fadeaway, or he'd drive the lane, or he'd give a couple head fakes, get David in the air, and drop in a little jump hook. He has so many moves, and he's so strong, that it's tough to figure out a way to play him.

When we won two straight titles in Detroit, I think it was more of a team thing. Houston had a good team around Olajuwon—Clyde Drexler and Robert Horry especially—but they got their shots because of him. Everything started with Hakeem and sort of fanned out to everybody else. With the Pistons, Isiah was the star, but every guy on that team could have been called a role player.

The *Sports Illustrated* article documenting my trip to Las Vegas in between the semifinals and finals—the one I talked about before—came out on May 29, right in the middle of our series with the Rockets. **I had nothing to do with the timing of the article, but I got blamed for it anyway.** I thought it was for way down the road, and then all of a sudden—boom!—there I am on the cover, wearing leather shorts and a dog collar. One of my birds was on my shoulder.

So there I go—*another big distraction.* There's another controversy. The Spurs started getting all pissed off, and they said, "There he goes again—he's in it for himself."

I had nothing to do with when that article came out. It became this huge problem, because it showed what I did with my time off the court. But that's nobody's business. They didn't realize that I could do those things; I could go to Vegas and still keep my mind straight about playing the games. I've been around enough to know how to handle that stuff. What I couldn't handle was those guys—especially Popovich—running around wondering what the hell I was doing with myself twenty-four hours a day.

Several people in the organization came up to me and asked me why I did that article. **"Why would you do that in the middle of the playoffs?"** That was their question, and they wouldn't listen when I told them I'd had nothing to do with the timing, and besides, it had nothing to do with how I was going to perform on the basketball court.

We were down two games to none, and they wanted to put it all on me. They sat there, like Avery Johnson, and trash-talked David, then they turned around in public and put everything on my head. **They wouldn't say a damn thing bad about David in public,** because they're all friends. Avery said it to his face—he was man enough to do that—but if it was me Avery was talking about, it would have been all over the papers the next day. Instead, because it was David, they kept it under wraps. It never came out that **AVERY HAD STOOD UP IN THE LOCKER ROOM AND SAID DAVID COULDN'T GET THE JOB DONE.**

They sat me out for part of Game 5 against Houston—a game we lost, 111–90—and afterward I just couldn't take it anymore. I went into the locker room and went off on the coach and the organization. I was so pissed at the way everything was being handled, and had been handled, that I couldn't keep it in anymore.

I told them what I thought of their coaching (it sucked) and their management (it sucked) and anything else I could think of. I went off on everybody. **I went off on Bob Hill. I told him he was a loser.** I told him he didn't know how to handle the playoff pressure. I said it was a crying shame that they could come out and say they wanted to win the series and then go out and pull **THE BONEHEAD SHIT THEY PULLED.** That was so stupid; I still get mad thinking about it.

When I went off, everyone on the team crowded around and tried to control me. When Avery did it, nobody did anything to him. He just spoke his piece and moved on. They couldn't let me do that.

I should have been playing forty minutes a game, every game. That was the only chance we had. Every coach in the league will tell you the same thing. You don't sit out a guy who's been in the playoffs all those years and knows how to handle every situation that comes up. To sit him down for twenty minutes is insane. Player rotation doesn't work in the playoffs.

I went off on Hill about the huddle thing too. If you're a

coach, and David Robinson doesn't want to join the huddle, are you going to make a big deal out of it? If Michael Jordan wants to sit over there by himself when he's not in the game, are you going to do something to punish him?

Everybody was trying to make a point, and **it was the *wrong time* to be making points.** They wanted to tell me I've got to be looking in Bob Hill's face every fucking second during a huddle. I heard what the man said; I knew the plays we were going to run. Even after I got to Chicago, I didn't look Phil Jackson in the face. I listened, but I wasn't staring into his eyes.

But I guess I have to look into Bob Hill's face and say, "Oh, yeah, Bob—that's what we should do." No. I know exactly where the ball's going. It's going straight to David. Do I have to look in Bob Hill's eyes to figure that out?

Like most coaches say, "As long as you do your job, I don't care what else you do." Most of them don't want to hear. As Chuck Daly used to tell me, "Go play, Dennis."

The biggest problem in San Antonio was Gregg Popovich, the general manager. He wanted to be the coach and the general manager. He stood around and held Bob Hill's hand every day, saying, "Okay, you've got to do this now. It's time for you to listen to me." If Hill didn't do it, Popovich would jump his ass, and so Hill would turn around and jump somebody else's ass. **Shit flows downhill, and it seemed I was always at the BOTTOM.**

Other than the playoffs I didn't have that much of a problem with Bob Hill. He was being used as much as I was. Popovich wanted to be the guy who tamed Dennis Rodman, and he tried to use Hill to do his dirty work. That was Popovich's big challenge. **Mr. Military was going to make me a good little boy, a good soldier.** He lost sight of everything else, and then when he decided he couldn't do anything with me, he badmouthed me and gave me away for next to nothing. Then he pretended it was good for the team.

I understand that the Spurs didn't give me the contract I

had signed in Detroit before the 1990 season. Nobody made me sign it, and it turned out to be a bad deal for me. It wasn't the Spurs' fault the market went crazy and I was left out in the cold. But none of that matters, because **THE SPURS SAID THEY WERE GOING TO GIVE ME $7 MILLION A YEAR, AND THEY WENT BACK ON THEIR PROMISE.** I could have lived with it if they had never said anything about the contract, but they did. I went into the office, and Popovich said, "We'll take care of you." Then he went to the papers and said he'd never said anything like that, and that he'd never heard about a new contract. *Would you be PISSED OFF if your boss treated you like this?* Of course you would. Everybody would.

After I left, the Spurs took care of Sean Elliott and David Robinson. They tore up their contracts and renegotiated to make sure those two stayed with the team through their whole careers. So what I was asking for wasn't something they'd never heard of, or thought of. I didn't want a contract that would keep me there my whole career. I know I'm not as young as those guys are—that's why I just wanted a two-year deal that would make up for all I'd given back to the team and the NBA. That wasn't there for me, though.

Everybody else can hold their tongue and hope for the best. I TELL IT THE WAY I FEEL IT, AND I DON'T GIVE A SHIT WHO GETS PISSED OFF.

In San Antonio it all came down to this: **I GOT SOLD OUT** by the players, the coaches, and the management. All up and down the organization I got sold out. I was out there on an island, an easy target for everything.

If some-thing went wrong, they had an easy answer. BLAME DENNIS.

thirteen

The Great Escape

The Circus Comes to Chicago

I don't think there's ever been a situation where people have sat down and talked with Dennis about what they want. We just made the effort to see where he was at, if he would commit to the team. He's willing, he's able, and we know he's going to come in and do the job.

—*Phil Jackson*

The Spurs traded me to the Chicago Bulls for center **WILL PERDUE, A GUY WITH NO GAME.** Straight up for Will Perdue, bro. That's how much San Antonio wanted to get rid of me.

I've been asked if I was insulted because they dumped me off for next to nothing, and my answer is this: I'm not insulted by it at all. The people who should be insulted are the Spurs. They should be insulted and embarrassed. **They could have traded me for BABE THE PIG** and I wouldn't have given a damn. I don't care what the Spurs got for me. I just wanted to get out of San Antonio.

After the trade some of my old teammates with the Spurs came out and backstabbed me. It always amazes me the way that works. A guy can play his ass off for a team, and then when he's traded or dumped, a bunch of people come out and say what a bad guy he was, or how he didn't do that much for the team.

In other words, they come out and say stuff they would never say to the person's face. But if they're going to trash me after I leave, then *I'm going to come out and tell it like it is.*

David Robinson said, "For us it was a zoo last year. Sometimes I felt we were in Hollywood. Now we're a basketball team again."

They've been saying that for ten years in San Antonio: "Now we're a basketball team." What the hell does that mean? We were not a basketball team when I was there? Were we not a basketball team when we had the best record in the NBA and went to the Western Conference Finals? And now I guess David Robinson thinks it's a basketball team again because he's got Will Perdue? **THAT'S SO FUCKING STUPID IT ISN'T EVEN FUNNY.**

They might be more of a basketball team **if David Robinson didn't freeze up every time they play a big game.** He might want to start there if he wants a basketball team.

Then there was Chuck Person. I never had a problem with Chuck Person in San Antonio. I probably said two words to Chuck Person in the year he was there, so how could I have a problem with him?

David Robinson says now they're a team? That's so fucking stupid.

After the trade Chuck Person says, "Chemistrywise, I feel we're already better. Everybody's going to be on time, everybody's going to be responsible."

All that's just fucking perfect **if you're running a Boy Scout camp.** Then it's great to have everybody lined up on time, wearing their uniforms and saluting the flag. But, as David Robinson knows, this is a *basketball team* we're talking about. What do you want from a basketball team? Everybody on time, smiling in the locker room, hugging everybody's wife? Or do you want a basketball player who knows what it's like to win and might teach you something about how to get where you want to go?

I couldn't believe it—Chuck Person slashing me after I left. Of all people, Chuck Person. He did nothing in the playoffs. The man shot about 30 percent in the playoffs, and **he has the BALLS to come out and RIP ME?**

If I was wrong, I'll come out and admit it. Yeah, there were some things I was wrong about. Maybe I took things too far. But did anybody else show up for those games against the Rockets? I'll ask Chuck Person: Did you show up? Could you hit a shot in the playoffs? No, you didn't show up, and you couldn't hit a shot. So **shut up.**

Chuck Person shot 42 percent from the field during the season. He's an offensive player—he doesn't rebound, he doesn't play much defense—and he averaged 10.8 points a game that season. So I'M SUPPOSED TO THINK HIS OPINION MATTERS?

I'll go head to head with any of these guys when it comes to performance on the basketball court during the playoffs—or anytime I was there.

This is what I can't stand about the people in this business. If you want to know why I'm so down on this sport and the people playing it and running it, this is the perfect example. The first thing anybody does is **LOOK AROUND FOR AN ASS TO KISS.**

Guys like Chuck Person looked around and decided the right thing for him to do after I left was to rip me. Every one of those guys knew what Popovich wanted to hear. He didn't want to hear that they'd made a shitty trade, that the team got worse when I left. He didn't want to hear that, so a guy like Chuck Person—to make himself look good—pops off about me.

They said one thing to my face, then turned around and backstabbed me. When I was there, Chuck Person would come up to me and say, "Hey, Dennis, I want to learn from you." Then they turn around and stay stupid shit about me in the paper so they can get in good with Popovich.

What does Chuck Person expect me to come out and say? I guess I'm supposed to say, "You're right, Chuck Person, I said bad things about you the whole time I was there—even though I said two fucking words to you the whole time I was there."

If you're going to talk about me, talk it to my face. ***DON'T GO BACKSTABBING ME SO YOU CAN TRY TO SAVE YOUR SORRY CAREER.*** Chuck Person can't come close to saying something bad about me, because he did nothing in the playoffs. The only good playoff he had was when he was playing for Indiana in 1991, when he averaged 26 points a game in five games against Boston. And even when he did that, he couldn't control himself. He was waving his arms to the fans and doing all this crazy bullshit, getting everybody in Boston pissed off at him—something I know about. That series was the only thing Chuck Person has in his whole career.

I don't care if those guys hate me or not. I'm not living my life for them. **YOU DIE, YOU DIE ALONE.** When my career's over, I'm not coming back to this game. I won't need those guys. I'd rather go back home and work for $6.50 an hour—back at the airport, even—than hang around this game looking for a broadcasting job. That's what all these guys want to do: hang around long enough to get a job as a broadcaster.

Those guys in San Antonio can KISS MY ASS, especially Popovich. He pulled a bunch of bullshit on me every step of the way. He wanted to "tame" me, then when he found out I wasn't his puppy dog, he set out to do whatever he could to drag my name through the mud in the NBA. And where did it get him? It got him Will Perdue, that's what. Maybe if he had been a little smarter and kept his mouth shut, he could have gotten something better.

The sad part is, they may have actually believed they were going to be better with Will Perdue. They said that he fit in better with the team—in their minds—because **he's more of a family man.** He doesn't go out and do the things I did. He'll do what they want him to do, when they tell him to do it, and that's what they want **down there in that white-ass, conservative-ass city.**

The way I see it, he'll be a great addition to the team picnics, and the dinners with the players and their wives, but he won't give them much on the floor.

Popovich said Bob Hill was thrilled with the trade, but I don't believe it. Bob Hill wanted me to stay. It wasn't Bob Hill who was trying to get rid of me. He's a basketball man, and he wanted me to stay because he knew what I did for the team. Through all the bullshit Bob Hill knew I was there to take the pressure off David. Now David is going to have to do a hell of a lot more in the regular season to keep that team on top. I'm not sure he can do it.

David Robinson is a great player, but I don't think he is going to rise to the level that Olajuwon has reached. I don't think there's a chance in hell, to be honest. Olajuwon is too damn good. He's in a zone of his own, especially in the playoffs, and I think it's very hard to put those two in the same category.

When you **LOOK AT WHAT HAS HAPPENED SINCE I GOT TO CHICAGO,** it's hard to believe the decision to make the trade became such a big production. After we got off to a record start and hit the All-Star break with a 42–5 record, all that talk of whether I would be able to fit in was forgotten—as it should have been. I think it proved something about me, and it showed just how badly San Antonio handled the situation. Now everybody's talking about this Bulls team being one of the best teams ever. I don't think we could have been part of that if I was the guy the Spurs said I was.

Thе trade to Chicago didn't come off until **the Bulls talked to just about every person who ever met me.** They were calling up everybody: former teammates, former coaches, friends— just about anybody they could track down. I know what they were trying to do, but it would have been better if they could have just looked at what I do on the basketball court and made their decision based on that.

Finally, when they were almost ready to make the deal, they called me back there and had me spend three days talking to Jerry Krause, the general manager, and other people in the organization. I was happy to come to Chicago, but I was also insulted that I had to go through this big examination and cross-examination to decide if I could play basketball for them. I just figured they didn't believe in Dennis Rodman unless I was sitting there, face to face, telling them the things they wanted to hear. I understand it, I guess, but it was demeaning to go through that.

There's one thing everyone should understand: **I LIKE MY CHARACTER.** The situation in San Antonio hurt my character around the league, and that's sad. I wouldn't have had to go through all that stuff in Chicago—and the Bulls wouldn't have thought it was necessary—if San Antonio hadn't gone out of its way to mark me as damaged goods.

After a while I just figured it was more of the same stuff I'd become used to the last few years. I wanted out of San Antonio bad enough that it almost didn't matter what I had to go through. The Bulls wanted me to tell them I didn't have any problems with their rules, and that I was going to make every effort to be on time and keep the distractions down. **Phil Jackson was cool.** He said, "These are the rules, and if there's anything here you don't think you can handle, then let us know."

Their rules were no different than the rules anywhere else. It was the same stuff—be on time, dress a certain way, represent the team in a certain way—that I'd heard a thousand times before. I didn't have a problem with any of it. They were different from San Antonio, though: If I was late in San Antonio, even thirty seconds late, they fined me $500 and made a big deal out of it. It was in the papers, it was on the news—everything, bro. But if you're late with the Bulls, Jackson fines you $5 and gives you a chance to erase it in a free-throw shooting drill. You get to pick two other guys to shoot against three players. I always pick Michael and Steve Kerr, so no matter how bad I shoot, there's still a chance I'll win.

The media in Chicago went wild when it came out that the Bulls were talking to me. There was all this public debate about "the character issue" with me, whether I would be—are you ready?—**a big distraction on the team.** San Antonio went out of their way to mark me as damaged goods, and that hurt what people thought of my character in the NBA. If it hadn't, the Bulls wouldn't have thought it was necessary to put me through all those interviews. But as far as I'm concerned, **YOU'RE NOT BUY-ING MY CHARACTER.** You're buying my ability to help the team win basketball games. Everything else is not important.

In my mind my character wasn't damaged by the two years I spent in San Antonio. In other people's minds it might have been, but it sure didn't change me. I think the Spurs just didn't appreciate what my character could bring to the team and the city.

It was reported that I stayed at Jerry Krause's house for the two days I was being interviewed in Chicago. That was wrong: I stayed in a hotel. **IT WASN'T LIKE A SLUMBER PARTY** or something; it was a business meeting.

The interview, which was at Krause's house, was mostly Krause talking a lot. I'm much smarter than he thought I was, but I guess because I didn't say much he thought he had to do a lot of talking. He didn't have to rattle off a thousand different things just to make one point, though. I understood everything from the beginning, but I guess they didn't think I did.

It was all really simple. It boiled down to one thing: **Did I want to be a Chicago Bull or not?**

I never once said, "Yes, I'd love to play in Chicago." That's not my style. They had to make that choice, whether I was worth the risk, as everyone put it. The call was theirs to make. I told them I'd play hard wherever I was, that I'd keep doing the things I'd done my whole career.

The Bulls realized some of the facts of my case: 1) I missed exactly one practice in 1994–95 with the Spurs; 2) I was upset with the way I had been lied to by the Spurs management when it came to contract negotiations; and 3) Popovich took it personally when he couldn't tame me, so he tried to make me look bad every chance he got. I guess that was good enough for the Bulls, because they decided the rewards would outweigh the risks.

I KNEW THE SCORE. I knew the Bulls needed someone to **come IN and DO the DIRTY WORK.** They became interested in me when they saw how much it hurt them to lose Horace Grant. He was very unappreciated here, because he was playing in the shadows of all these great scorers. He wasn't appreciated until Michael came back and they realized what this team could have done if Horace hadn't signed with Orlando. Then everybody, all of a sudden, said Horace Grant *had* been the key to that team. They might have been right. Horace Grant *had* been the heart of that team; every team needs someone to come in and clean up everybody's mess, make life easier for the stars. That's what I've done my whole career.

Horace Grant is very tough mentally, just like me. We're very similar players, and that's why we've had some great battles in the past. He's one of the guys I respect the most because **WHEN I PLAY HIM I ALWAYS**

END UP GETTING MAD. When I get mad, it makes me better. It helps me get my mind straight.

There aren't many people who doubt the Bulls could have won everything in '95 if Horace Grant had still been on that team. They needed to fill that hole that he left behind, and they knew I was the guy who could do it. No matter how many times they talked to me, no matter how many times they talked to Jack Haley about me, there was no way they could avoid that: they needed me in Chicago if they were going to get back to where they'd been when they won three NBA titles in a row.

MICHAEL JORDAN AND SCOTTIE PIPPEN HAD TO APPROVE THE TRADE that brought me to Chicago, and that was fine with me. If one of them had a big problem, I would have gone somewhere else.

Milwaukee

Jordan and Pippen had to approve the trade.

was interested, and I'd heard they were willing to restructure my contract to make me a happy man. But I think Jordan and Pippen realized I wasn't coming in to be the big man on the Bulls. I go out and play my role; **I'M NO THREAT TO THOSE GUYS.** All I can do is help them, make their jobs easier.

After I got to the Bulls, **Michael and Scottie said they had some concerns about me** coming to the team, but those concerns went away in training camp. Michael said nobody had ever picked up the Bulls' complicated offense as fast as I did—not even him. Everybody was impressed—and surprised, I guess—by my basketball knowledge. ***MAYBE THEY HADN'T BEEN WATCHING ME THE PAST NINE YEARS.***

I never once said, "Oh, great, I get to play with Michael Jordan and Scottie Pippen." I respect their talents, and I enjoy being on the floor with them, but I'm not in awe of them. I'm not starstruck because I'm on the same team.

I went through all of training camp without saying two words to Michael Jordan off the court. That's the way I am with everybody. ***I really don't talk to anybody.*** It doesn't matter where I am or who I'm playing with. You could put me on Miami or Minnesota and it would be the same way. It doesn't mean I don't get along with Michael. We both have the same model Ferrari, so we've talked about that. And we talk about basketball. We all get along on the court, and that's where it matters.

I think this Chicago team can be as good as the Pistons teams, but I'll always have a soft spot for those teams in Detroit. We had everything there, and it was special for me because that was where I started and learned the game.

The other thing you have to mention when you talk about this Bulls team is the league. The NBA is down right now. There are so many terrible teams out there, it's hard to say how the Bulls would compare to the other great teams. All I know is, they better do something about this league before it's too late.

We're in a pretty cool position in Chicago, with three of

the biggest attractions in basketball. The attention we get is incredible. Every city, every game, every single day. We had to have police escorts every place we went, even places like Sacramento. It was unlike anything the NBA had seen.

Everybody knows Michael Jordan can go out and score 50 points. If he gets in a zone, it's over. It's amazing to watch the way some players find the creases and slash to the basket, and that's **WHAT AMAZES ME THE MOST ABOUT MICHAEL.** You can talk all you want about the way he jumps and the dunks, but the people who know basketball are more impressed with the way he finds his way to the hoop—the way he can always get a shot off. Scottie Pippen is that way, too. He impressed the hell out of me when I first got to Chicago, and I think **HE'S MORE IMPRESSIVE WHEN YOU'RE PLAYING WITH HIM THAN AGAINST HIM.**

When Scottie Pippen first came into the league, I told anybody who would listen that he was going to be **one of the BEST FORWARDS ever to play the game.** I could tell from his athletic ability and the different things he could do—he's a great defensive player, he's a damn good rebounder, and he can get his shot off anywhere, anytime. He was no surprise to me.

I think *TONI KUKOC* is the guy who was most affected by the trade. He **went from being the best player on the whole continent of Europe to being the fourth best player on his own team.** I'm not saying he was overwhelmed when I showed up, but he has to understand that with the kind of team they've put together here, it doesn't matter who gets the glory. This team will free him up to do whatever he has to do; he just needs to understand that and get his mind right about the game. **We'll cover up for Kukoc's mistakes.** He's a great shooter, so he can shoot 15 times a game and score 16 or 17 points a game, easy. Kukoc can take over the Vinnie Johnson, instant-offense role on this team.

Everything with the Bulls comes back to Jordan, though. Always. There were all these questions about whether Jordan made me feel comfortable being a part of the team in Chicago. I have to explain that it's really not like that. I don't care if I'm comfortable, and **IT'S NOT HIS JOB TO MAKE ME FEEL COMFORTABLE.** I don't care if everyone likes me. In fact, I might be a better player if I'm not totally comfortable.

When you move from one city to another, you have to feel wanted. I felt wanted in Chicago from the beginning from a basketball sense, because I knew exactly what I was coming here to do. I knew what they needed, and I knew I could give it to them. They weren't interested in taming me or keeping me in line. That's the only feeling of comfort I needed.

Michael was quoted as saying he thought I could average 10 or 11 rebounds on this team. I guess I could have taken that as an insult—10 or 11 rebounds is a good half for me— but I knew what he meant. He meant that I wouldn't have to get more than 10 or 11 a game to make a difference on this team. He wouldn't come out and say I could average 17 or 18 a game—or that I *needed* to average that many— because that would have put unnecessary pressure on me. If I was a guy who might feel pressure, which I'm not.

I missed a month at the beginning of the season with a strained calf muscle, but I was leading the league in rebounding as soon as I got enough games under me. **I went into the All-Star break leading the league in rebounding,** ahead of the next guy by almost three boards a game, **but I still didn't make the All-Star team.**

Let's be reasonable about this, bro. Should I have made the All-Star team? Of course I should have. I wasn't the only one saying this, either. Michael Jordan was saying it, the television announcers, like Danny Ainge, were saying it. Everybody knew it, but the Eastern Conference coaches decided I didn't deserve it.

Here's why: The game was in San Antonio, bro. Could you imagine the scene if I went back to San Antonio for the All-Star Game? They didn't want any part of that. It would have been too perfect for me. I would have gone down there and taken all the attention away from the NBA's chosen ones, and there was no way they were going to let that happen. They wouldn't give me the satisfaction of going back down there under those circumstances. It had nothing to do with what happens on the court, but I guess I should be used to that by now.

The people in Chicago weren't leading the rush to join the Dennis Rodman Fan Club before the trade. In fact, they hated me when I was with Detroit.

We had some great battles with the Bulls in those days. After we took over the Eastern Conference from Boston, the Bulls were the next team to challenge us. They eventually took over from us, winning three in a row after we won two in a row, and there was **some bad blood on the court** every time we got together.

Sometimes, there was **REAL BLOOD ON THE COURT.** One time it was *Scottie Pippen's blood*—and I was the reason it got there. In the 1991 Eastern Conference Finals I sort of pushed him from behind and he landed chin-first in the first row of the stands. He got a nasty cut—the scar's still there—and I got a $5,000 fine.

So I guess it was natural when I got traded to Chicago that people wondered how the hell I was going to fit in to a city and a team that had hated me for so long.

The way I see it, this is another example of people not understanding how athletes think.
I don't expect Scottie Pippen to forgive me for what I did to him. I don't expect him to forget about it either. It's just the same when someone does something to me; sometimes you don't forgive them, but you can go out and play with them. My past history against the Bulls was not even an issue with Jordan and Pippen, or anybody else on that team.

We played each other hard back in those Pistons-Bulls days, and we all knew the score with me coming in. We knew that now we were going to play just as hard—this time together.

There was always respect there, even when we were fighting each other like cats and dogs. That's why those games were so great. We wouldn't have played as hard against somebody we didn't respect—we wouldn't have had to. So for anybody to think I was going to walk into that locker room my first day as a Bull and **GO RIGHT UP TO SCOTTIE AND SAY, "HEY, BRO, I'M SORRY"**—that's crazy. It's not like I was going to do that and he was going to accept my apology and shake my hand, and then everything would be perfect. It doesn't work that way—it doesn't need to work that way.

I did a lot of things back in those "Bad Boy" days. It was all part of the package. I do the same things today, but I think I'm a little smarter about it. I pick my spots. After that incident with Pippen, I think he took himself out of the game. I don't think I took him out of his game; I think he did it by himself. **I think he got a little** *freaked out by me.* I think he started playing the game thinking, *This goddamn guy's always on my ass.* He couldn't do anything.

All of a sudden he came down with a migraine headache. A lot of people think it wasn't true, but I think it was true. **MAYBE HE HAD** RODMAN ON THE BRAIN. If you've got a headache, go play. But he had a migraine, and that's severe. If you have one of those, you can't play because you can't concentrate.

I really don't think I gave him the migraine. I think the media did, the way they were on his ass that whole series. I was just doing my job on the floor, making him think about what he had to do the next day to make up for what he was doing at the time. Back then I was shutting everybody down, not just Scottie Pippen.

I chose number 91 when I got to Chicago, just to be different. The league had to approve it—the league has to approve any number above 55—and they did. Surprise. Maybe they figured they'd throw me a bone. I chose 91 because I couldn't have my old number, 10—Bob Love wore it there and they retired it. And nine and one add up to 10, so what the hell? Plus, what are the first two numbers you dial in an emergency? See what I'm saying? **WHO DO YOU CALL TO PUT OUT THE FIRE?**

Our first preseason game with the Bulls was in Peoria, of all

What are the first TWO NUMBERS you dial in an emergency?

places. It was like a rock group on tour the way people crowded around us and screamed and yelled. As Phil Jackson told his son after they traded for me, **"We don't have to go to the circus. It came to us."**

During that first game, **I had a little temper tantrum.** The replacement referees were way out of their league, and they made a foul call on me that I didn't like. I took the ball and threw it against the shot clock on top of the backboard; naturally, I got a technical foul.

One year with Bob Hill had trained me to look over at the coach as soon as I did something. He would be standing up yelling at somebody to go in and get me out of the game. He'd have this awful look on his face, like **the world was going to end because I did something stupid.** In this case Bob Hill would have had somebody at the scorer's table checking in for me before the ball landed on the floor. Then he would have brought me over to the sidelines to tell me all the things I shouldn't be doing on the basketball floor.

So I looked over at Phil Jackson, and I couldn't believe it. **The man was laughing.** He was kicking back in his chair, and he was laughing. I thought this was cool. Phil Jackson knows the game. He knows I can go out and spark a team with the outrageous things I do. He knows all the ins and outs, all the angles, and he knows I'm going to bring something to the team that it needs.

Phil Jackson played, and he played during the late 1960s and early '70s, when not everyone followed the same program. He was one of them. He admitted to taking LSD, and now he's into all this Zen stuff when it comes to coaching. He's not a Marine; he's a human being.

I found out from the start, he's going to let me go. He's not as worried about distractions, because look at who he's been coaching all these years. The Bulls know about distractions, and they know how to play through them. **If I go out and have a sex change, he might wonder: What the hell?** But other than that, he's going to let the team play the way it needs to play.

I missed twelve games early in the season after I strained a calf muscle. I've done that before, and I knew right away I was going to miss a month. It's like taking your car to the mechanic; after he tells you what the problem is, he says it's going to take four days to fix it. He knows, because he's done it before. My calf is the same way. I know my body.

The Bulls didn't pressure me to come back. The day before I did come back, I practiced hard—nearly full speed—for close to two hours. So all the reporters naturally asked Jackson whether I was going to play the next night, at home against the New York Knicks.

Here's what Jackson said: "It's just Dennis. At this point I'm not sure he knows when he'll be ready. If he says, 'I'm just not in shape to play with the kind of energy I have to have on the court,' that's understandable."

I played that night against the Knicks and had 20 rebounds. We had a terrible first half, and Michael, Scottie, and I led us back to win in the second half. The people in Chicago were way into everything I did. I made a basket off a feed from Michael to bring us within a point at the end of the third quarter. I was fouled, too, and **as I walked to the foul line Michael and I hugged.** The place went berserk; the people were realizing **what this team was capable of doing with me in the lineup.**

Whenever someone would ask Phil Jackson if anything I've done surprised him, he would always say, **"Yeah, it surprises me that he needs a special tool to take his pressurized earrings out."** That's what I mean about him: He's taking everything in stride.

When I looked over there during that first exhibition game and saw him laughing as the ref was slapping a T on me, and when I read what he said about me coming back from the injury, I couldn't believe it. I wasn't expecting that. I wasn't ready for that. Somebody understands? **A coach who understands?** One thought came to my mind:

Finally.

255

PHOTO CREDITS